MUDFISH 18

MUDFISH 18

POETRY - ART - FICTION

Edited by Jill Hoffman

Box Turtle Press/Attitude Art, Inc.
184 Franklin Street, New York, New York 10013

Editor: **Jill Hoffman**
Associate Editors: **Lawrence Applebaum, Jennifer Belle, Stephanie Emily Dickinson, Doug Dorph, Marina Rubin, Matt Sapio, and Paul Wuensche**
Assistant Editors: **Laura Hetzel, Zoe Contros Kearl, Maeve Nolan**
Business Development: **Jack Herz**

Jacket and book design: **Anne Lawrence**
Cover: **Jill Hoffman** "Frank," 2014. Oil on canvas, 36" x 36"
Back Cover: **Jill Hoffman** "Out All Night," 2014. Oil on canvas, 36" x 36"
Typeset in Futura

Box Turtle Press/Attitude Art, Inc. is a not-for-profit corporation.
Contributions to Mudfish (Box Turtle Press/Attitude Art, Inc.) are welcome and tax-deductible.

To subscribe, send $20 for one issue (plus $3.50 shipping) or $40 for two year subscription (shipping & handling included). Make checks payable to: Box Turtle Press, 184 Franklin Street, New York, NY 10013
Distributed by: Small Press Distribution, 1341 Seventh Street Berkeley, CA 94710-1409, Ingram Periodicals Inc.,18 Ingram Blvd., LaVergne, TN 37086
and Ubiquity Distributors, 607 Degraw St., Brooklyn, NY 11217
Copyright December 2014 Box Turtle Press, 184 Franklin St., NY, NY 10013, 212.219.9278, Mudfishmag@aol.com; Mudfishbooks@gmail.com; www.mudfish.org

MUDFISH 18

TABLE OF CONTENTS

To view art in full color visit www.mudfish.org

ART

WINNER OF THE 11TH MUDFISH POETRY PRIZE
CHOSEN BY CHARLES SIMIC

Elisabeth Murawski

WAKING ALONE ON SUNDAY MORNING

The bed warm, the house cold,
the sun bold as Paul

setting out for Rome
and certain death,

I surrender to languor.
The birds have flown south.

A dog barks to be let in.
Each year, hearing

for the first time
the double coo that gave

the bird its name, Wystan Hugh
would note the moment

in his diary, calling it
holy, the return

of the ordinary
knocking him to his knees.

Elisabeth Murawski

The two-note wonder
fortified,

like two blue clouds
in a child's drawing

of the sky, white
because it doesn't have to be.

Laura Hetzel, "Maeve," 2011. photo

OTHERWISE

We each name olive groves, the dead, the skies.
Not one cup or stone is negotiable.
We cannot go on living, otherwise.

We claim the first rain, the last almond, allies.
The situation is untenable.
We each name olive groves, the dead, the skies,

accuse each other of bad faith, quick lies.
We arrive empty-handed at the table
and do not speak. We salt our wounds. Otherwise,

life goes on. For our children we'd give our eyes.
We, too, as children heard the tale of Babel,
how we named olive groves, the dead, the skies,

mulberries, wild hyssop, without compromise:
for a sweet tomorrow pledged in rubble.
We are told it cannot be otherwise.

We watch schools burn, let acrid black smoke rise.
We might learn together, through our troubles,
new names of olive groves, the dead, the skies,
common words with which to speak otherwise.

2ND HONORABLE MENTION
Cornelia Hoogland

SCENES FROM A MARRIAGE

A dog.

Out of the blue
a dog bound between us in bed –
licked our faces
open

       while outside
frost rang circles
round the stems of rushes
on the river. Ice
necklaces.

A breathing panting
red-tongued dog –
a carnivore.

And then it snowed.
Dogs love snow.
They jump up on all fours
as if to stop the falling
or be part of it.

Fine drifty snow –
a duvet plumping
its feathers
over the shook pines.

Blowing snow, fierce –
a film shot from a plane high
above everything.
It took longer than opera.

The undersides of the storm
were roads
leading to towns
gnarled as the subterranean roots
of silver-leaved trees
rattled by
winds greater
than the camera's eye.

The near miss of the heart.

The dog strained at its leash
or was it
what we together
became
that pulled
us over the fields.

Robert Steward

FREELANCING

from Arnold2

Sonia's meticulous plan is disturbed when her sister Blanche announces she has a broken tooth problem. There will be no meeting today to discuss Sonia's love life; sometimes called her *War on Men*. Off the phone she checks her mental diary and sees a yawning gap between now and her date with Arnold at noon. Time to visit the library, or think pleasant thoughts? No, she'll take a long shower and *walk* the mile and a half it takes to get to the Beehive Café. A refreshing idea. Sonia's life is usually all about taxicabs; underwear malfunctions, instant sex. But the weather is beautiful. And that's new too.

Swinging along the Thames Embankment in one of her casually expensive short-skirted outfits (a gift from boyfriend No. 4) Sonia catches a reflection of her sunlit red hair in a car window and feels blessed. She decides to take the scenic route to the Beehive via Fuller's Yard – a large stretch of dappled lawn with giant rustling sycamores that seem to reach the sky.

But even as she steps through the gate, the tempo of her morning stroll is ruffled by a big man who is striding towards her across the grass, lowering his face to stare directly into her eyes. The fleshy cheeks and over-ripe smile suggest he's hoping his verbal skills will come to his rescue if everything else fails. "Out for a breath of fresh air, I see," he says. "Very charming, if I may say so." He gives Sonia the usual admiring once over. He's maybe forty. Bulky in the middle. Thinning on top. Somewhat disheveled. A familiar type —repellent but interesting? Nar, nar, she thinks. "Not today please, but…"

"I never talk to strangers in filthy sneakers," she says, removing her dark glasses and looking down at his feet. During her recent shower she swore she'd be careful today. But one provocative moment can upset any best-laid plan, as they say. You can call Sonia a *whore* if you want, or just a common or garden variety slut, but she prefers Blanche's term:

"Freelancer." Working off the books, under the table. Men are just men. You have to play with them in the street like the eager jumping puppy dogs they are.

The big man shrugs in an amenable way and casually removes each sneaker using the opposite foot, a Vaudevillian gesture, she realizes. "How's that, my dear?" he asks hoping for approval. "I never speak in public to a man in socks," says Sonia. Then he goes ha, ha, ha, and removes his socks, laying them almost gracefully on the sneakers. His feet have mysterious blue Gorgonzola veins running in them. To Sonia's amusement and relief his toe-nails are beautifully pedicured. There's a note of theatrical cheek about him. Maybe he isn't the smelly wanker he seemed to be at first.

"Can I introduce myself," he says, hand extended. She grips him by the fingers, not the palm. A lady-like move for some, but her grip has this guy wincing. He shrieks in a manly way and goes red in the face. Released, he shakes his hand like it's an old washcloth, and goes ho, ho, ho like Santa Claus. He knows he's been tested, like the chimpanzees that get their ears tugged by future chimpanzee lovers. "That was funny!" he says, "By the way, I'm Gerard Stanley Price. Computer geek by day, raconteur by night. Call me Gerry, if you like. What happens now, love?"

"You die from the toxic pigeon shit you're standing in, Gerry."

"That's all?"

"You can always go to hell to, of course."

"Cup of coffee, ten minutes, max," he says.

Sonia glances at her watch. "Pick your stuff up," she says.

Various forms of invisible erotica churn in Gerry's head as he drools across the table at Ericka. (Sonia introduced herself as "Ericka" when they entered the coffee shop. That tag has been her *nom de romance* for years. Chosen by her faithful sister, Blanche, of course.)

They sit in a corner. Farouk, the waiter, comes over to take their order. Gerry seems to be thinking. Perhaps he's trying to figure out his approach. Over his shoulder a cheaply framed picture of an exquisite French village —

Castelnaud-la-Chapelle — hangs mysteriously on the wall. Ericka has a vision in which she and Gerry take an extended sojourn to the South of France. She is returning from the local street market to the gorgeous old house Gerry has rented, carrying a bunch of perfect flowers. Gerry is still in bed, asleep after a hard night last night. His head is covered. His feet stick out from under the quilt. His beautiful toenails gleam in the mid-morning sun. She puts the flowers down and kisses the toes one by one. Gerry is still dreaming. And Ericka is in love. The truly great thing about Gerry is his improbability. If you have the looks of an Ericka, no one dares to laugh at you for hanging out with a middle-aged jerk with a gout problem. And no one laughs at him either.

Ericka stirs her coffee. It tastes awful. "Well now Gerry Price," she says brightly, "Tell me all about Gerry Price."

"Oh yeah, that troubled and sensitive soul, eh? Ha ha," goes Gerry. "He's a decent, caring bloke, he likes to think. Married once. Big mistake. Wrong mix. No kids. Single now. Divorced eight years. Nice ex-wife, Lily. She's very nice indeed. Bygones are bygones. No rancor. Just…well, you know…" He straightens up. "So, enough about me, sprocket," he says, "In the event that WE ever do something — together I mean, it'd be totally different. We'd learn from what life has taught us. Settle down. Relax. Hang out. You'd be my sprocket. I'd be your Gerry Boy. How's that sound, love?"

'"Fascinating," Ericka says. She enjoys grown up fun, but it comes with a penalty if you're a woman. You have put up with all the bloody Poppets, Pringles and Sprocket nicknames that "mature" men sprinkle all over you like party glitter.

"Excellent. Now it's time for *your* story Ericka?" says Gerry.

"I'm in marketing. Insurance firm. I hang out in Islington. Born in Ipswich." It's as if she's been captured on the field of battle and must reveal the absolute minimum. She doesn't mention her reputation as a man killer, an unscrupulous opportunist, or a gal with super great legs.

"Ipswich? My brother lives there," says Gerry.

"Huh?" Ericka looks away. She's never been to Ipswich in her life.

How did Blanche come up with Ipswich? She reaches for a Kleenex to do something delicate with her left eyelash.

Gerry changes the subject. Nodding, he says: "Lots of friends, right?"

"A few," she says modestly. Gerry disguises the slightly lascivious gaze. "So this is where it goes now, poppet," he says, trying to take some kind of charge.

"Where *what* goes now, Gerry?" Sonia smiles amiably.

"I mean our fortuitous meeting and its important implications."

"Oh that! Of course! Tell me more."

"Remember, you insisted I take my sneakers off? Fair enough. Now you have to order me to strip 'till I'm naked. You too, 'course. Then it's down to business. Across the street. Nice flat. Very handy. Clean sheets. Not a palace, but nice. Just you and me. Twenty minutes. We're done! I'm off to work and I know you're a busy girl."

Sonia sips her coffee. "But Gerry," she says, "I'm not speaking for all women, but I happen to have feelings. It's not smash and grab with every girl. Know what I mean? We need the cigarette, the flowers, the reassuring words..."

Gerry grabs a little packet of high fructose corn syrup and tries to read the microscopic warnings on the back. What can he fucking do? Holy shit. Answer: go for broke: "Okay," he says. "Let me put it this way, sprocket. Imagine *you and me* knocking about the local markets on a Saturday morning, picking up stuff for the weekend. A pound of lamb shank. A dozen eggs. I love chicken cacciatore. Love garlic too. The Hair & Hounds, 'round the corner, has karaoke every Wednesday night. Lovely sing-along, you know? No cover charge! We'd have a couple of toddlers in time. I love kids, just in case you wondered. We'd buy a nice little house. Settle down. Grow our own vegtables. Buy a caravan and ride out to Gravesend for the weekend."

"Mmmm!" goes Ericka.

"Yes! So now let's take a little trip across the road and get to know each other. We can discuss the other stuff later." Ericka twirls a lock of red hair. "I need to tell you something, Gerry." He jerks forward, all hairy ears.

"What?"

"I hate karaoke."

"Oh, of course, that's optional," he says. "We could do the monthly barn dance at the Community Centre instead. Both hands are back-peddling now in an Italian gesture that means — '*Life is a mystery to be explored, not understood.*'

"Okay," he continues, "Suppose we spend some time together across the street (no rush, 'course) then meet tonight to talk about our future." He's seeing a quick fuck now. A slow dinner later. It's set out in his mind, tableaux style. Candles, naked breasts, whacks on the bottom (his) posh nosh, Ericka sipping champagne. Intimacies exchanged. Ericka insists on paying her share.

He looks carefully at Ericka.

Her face has turned into a slow question mark.

Gerry panics. His babbling tongue has ruined everything. What a fool! Doesn't he know by now? Minimize the verbal! Either it works or you get punched in the nose. Fair enough. Rule one: *Talk straight. Move fast. Run for cover.*

"I'm not into relationships," Ericka says. Gerry's face goes pretend sad. "I'm more of a freelancer, if you know what I mean. To come to the point, I charge five hundred an hour. No checks. No wire transfers. But you, Gerry, have twenty minutes. I won't steal from you. That's my minimum, sorry."

Gerry shrinks into his chair. "That's it?" he asks bleakly.

"Yes, Gerry. But here's a token for you." She gets up and makes a move on his rubbery face intended as a non-committal peck. But she has to swerve to the left to avoid lips that curl toward her like a cartoon serpent. "Bye Gerry," she says, "Delicious coffee! Thanks."

Gerry sits for a moment, then wanders to the counter where Farouk is clattering cups and saucers. "She's quite the looker, that one," Farouk says, "if you don't mind me sayin'." Gerry nods without comment. Through the window, Ericka's fetching rear end recedes into the distance.

Ericka walks along Farringdon Road, but after a hundred yards, doubts set in. She stops to polish her sunglasses. Then spins on her heels and returns to the coffee shop. Gerry is talking to the earthy-looking boy who served them a few minutes ago. Heads low and close. They have the guilty eyes of men talking about frigid whores, whatever that could possibly mean. Gerry senses Sonia's presence and spins on his stool. Farouk disappears. His exit gets Sonia's attention. Nice looking man, she's thinking. Perfect skin tones. Nice body.

"I want to say I'm sorry, Gerry," says Ericka.

"Let's hop into bed then?" He gives her a rueful smile. "Or not, as the case may be."

.   "You should be mad at me," she says, "I'm partially wrong in the head, you know."

"Partially?" Gerry's thinking: "What about totally?" But his pretentions in amateur psychiatry are alerted. She won't get into bed with him. But she might lie on his couch. Not that he's a pro, everything he knows about psychiatry he read on the back of the Collins Classic edition, "Mind over Matter." It was in the hands of a nice looking Asian woman he sat next to on the bus a week ago.

"I don't care," says Gerry. She's the nutcase, not me. He's been right from the get go.

"Well now we're square," Ericka says almost tenderly. It's refreshing for her to be with a guy who doesn't live and die by her every word. "We can still fuck a-course," Gerry says. A shout of laughter leaps from her body and the red hair flies like a flame. It's over. Gerry knows that. But just talking to Ericka — making her laugh out loud especially – is doing more for him with Farouk and the others than if they had piled into Farouk's unmade bed. She's clever, he's thinking, keeping me off balance, teasing me to death.

"Tell me," she says, "When you're hitting on a woman, which do you respect more. A clear "yes" or a clear "no"?

"Professional secret," says Gerry, looking at her skeptically. She might be trying to maneuver him into friendship — the worst outcome possible for Gerry. "Are you fishing?" he says, half kidding, half hoping. Ericka smiles. In her other life she knows how to fish, casually casting her lines into great big oceans of men, landing barracuda, blue shark, colossal squid, golden carp, iridescent tropical guppy. Gerry is a couple of kippers. But kippers have a particular taste you can't forget.

"Okay," she says, "Tell me. What exactly is a sprocket?"

"Something you keep in the garden shed," he says, "You don't know what the hell it's for. You think about it once in a while, perhaps affectionately."

"Is that what you wanted to do with me?"

"Yes."

"Ha! Suppose I told you my name is not Ericka—would you be upset?"

"Yes."

"Sorry to tell you but from now on I'm Sonia."

"Pleased to meet you, Sonia," Gerry says with a deadpan smile.

"Now Gerry; is Gerry your real name?"

"'Course not."

"Ah, ha. So when were you planning to tell me you are still married?"

"Who told you?"

"It's easy to detect a pale indent on a ring finger."

Gerry looks out of the window. "Guilty as charged," he says.

"How many kids?"

"Two girls, five and seven." His nose hairs bristle with fatherly pride. "The little one's a darling," he says, "The other's a pain in the bloody neck sometimes."

"Like you?"

"The girls aren't bald, otherwise they are like me."

"Do you give them pedicures?"

"No. That's my personal treat. Confirms my masculinity. Wife disagrees. She says I'm an effeminate blubber boy. Can you believe that?"

"Yes I can. What's her name?"

"Ruby."

"That's beautiful." Sonia looks at Gerry with the face of love. Not for Gerry exactly. But at times any crumb of life Sonia comes across reminds her of Arnold. And Arnold reminds her of everything else. Even the chip in the coffee cup she has in her hand. "Very nice coffee," she tells Farouk who hovers, smiles, and disappears.

Sonia is meeting Arnold in half an hour. She's heard of being true to one man. But it just never seems to work out that way.

"Gerry, do you really live across the street?"

"I have the key to a flat across the street."

"Who lives there?"

"Farouk."

"Really?" Ericka says, "Is he married?"

"I'd rather you asked him yourself if you don't mind."

Paul Wuensche, "Houseboats on the Thames," 2014. Oil on canvas, 40" x 32"

Lindsay Ahl

NOUMENA

Put your hand
in the track
of a leopard, and he will know
you are following.

Meet your husband
in a conference room on 64th
and Broadway to have crazy
sex overlooking the tiny cars below
and he will know
you are as clear as the glass
window you stand before — no where
to go but down.

Hang a necklace on the door
for your daughter (a door
you are no longer
allowed through) and when
she finds it — after
school, before her mother gets home —
she will know (eventually)
that you taught her
how to move as invisibly
as the wind.

Lindsay Ahl

WILDING

I dedicate this poem to the Central Park Runner
(She disliked the term Jogger. Wild

Grace kept her alive: she still runs). One of seven people
Attacked that night, raped and beaten

Almost to death — her skull fractured so severely
Her eye hung from its socket.

I love the word *wilding*, which is what the media
Initially called it — what gangs did — assaulting

Strangers. On the West Side Bridle Path, near the back wall —
I once saw a man up against a woman, a flash

Of her exposed thigh —
And in the Brambles — I once saw roving men

Meet each other. To be hungered after, longed for — I wanted
That. Never afraid of the park, I wasn't afraid

Of wilding, the word too pretty, and the park
With its rocks and trees and pathways, sloping and green,

And every year an unpredictable week in April
(She was running in April –),

By the reservoir in spring, thousands of white petals
On trees hundreds of years old, bloom

And then fall in a small paradise. I have come here
To see the cherry blossoms — the row by the East Side Bridle Path —

I raise my son, only four days old — *Look*, I tell him
(Turning around beneath petals

Filled with light) — if only those boys knew —
This too

Is a wilding —

Farrell Brickhouse, "Descended Staircase," 2014.
Oil on carpeted wood panel, 23" x 19 7/8"

Joseph Battani

PENN STATION

At a sink
in the Penn Station Men's Room
bathes an unclothed man. Though
ancient and reeking wondrous,
his garments pooled in smoke
on the blue tile floor, he bears
the lustrous body of a maiden.
Water spouts from his nose,
lipslash, sprigs of hair
upcurled like white pine shavings,
tiny breasts and pouting abdomen,
the long black saddle of his flanks.
Bells chime. Trains flash
in tunnels below. He rains —
travelers in the grand hurry
of ablution gape — never
once opening his eyes.

Coco de Casscza
ONCE

thirty years ago
I came into Penn Station
at one in the morning

past twisted bodies
in the tunnels
like the *Inferno*

thinking
I'd arrive
to see the dawn
not wait the night
not having budgeted
a bed at the Y

Everyone in the station
is gathered inward
by a circle of benches
under a featureless ceiling
is desperate or crazy
drug-addled
screaming
or the children of these

Only the children
and two more of us
rest with aplomb
the children sleeping

or dazedly playing
we two
youths
sit opposite
each other
a posed photo in my memory
a fellow
reading Italo Calvino
I Fanny Burney's *Evelina*

Next day
on the way to the Met
I lunched at the Carlyle
for what the Y would have cost
because I'd resolved
to eat at the next nice place

If youth made sense
we wouldn't remember
with terrified pleasure

Lawrence Applebaum

CYPRESS HILL CEMETERY

You asked if I would take you to see
your parents. The J train was bleaker
than a death scene with two bus rides.
Bob had taken you in the past, but he
was dead now. You told me Piet
Mondrian, Eubie Blake and Jackie
Robinson were buried there, among
others, you laughed. I could feel them
in the rust of the wrought iron. The
Islamic archway was a wave over our
heads as we passed the gate. We
walked for ten minutes. There
were steep hills. I couldn't believe so
many people were buried on a slant.
We had to hold onto each other when
we slid down the steepest hill on
stepping-stones that felt like head
stones. It was like walking on
Mondrian's Broadway Boogie-Woogie,
only downhill and a little bit sideways.
Your parents were at the bottom
tucked away in a bed, shaded by a
maple, with a railing in front like a brass
headboard. It felt like they were sitting
upright, on a terrace, happy to see
you. You asked me to take a picture of
their stones in case you never went back.
You never did. On the way out, we

peeped into some beautiful mausoleums that were like brownstone dollhouses. As a surprise you took me to see Mae West's tomb. Her name carved alone in marble was glamorous. Then to the Collyer Brothers, Homer and Langley — my mother had always told me I lived like the Collyer Brothers because I collected things. Later we went to Little Poland for dinner and when the dessert came you asked the waitress for an extra sprinkling of cinnamon over your rice pudding. Life's too short you told me, you were only ninety then.

Lawrence Applebaum, "Gertrude," photo

Anna Halberstadt

VILNIUS DIARY

The language I thought I had forgotten
rises from the depth of childhood
gradually revealing layers
of faded Technicolor dreams.
First day of school
terror and swallowed tears
in the class where instructions are given
in a language I understand
but do not speak.
Bouquets of gladioli and asters
obscuring faces, black aprons
and white lace collars on brown
school uniforms.
Older kids with red pioneer ties
taking us into the classroom.
Panic mixes with guilt
in the heart of a seven
year old little trooper.
Dark hallways of the school
with Germanic military order
children being taught how to report
their classmates breaking rules.
During recess in the spring
running out into the school yard
being pushed around by tall merginos
in the much dreaded basketball
but excelling in gymnastics and ballet.
In seventh grade sitting by the window in a black turtleneck

reading or drawing doodles on notebook margins.
Despising girly pursuits of knitting
crocheting and baking pies
but secretly practicing the dance moves
to Paul Anka's "You are my Destiny"
and the Beatles "Yesterday."
When I come here once again
this city is half real - half a hallucination
walks with father
through streets of linden trees
dear ghosts that live in neglected courtyards
with assorted knick knacks
and pots with red geranium on windowsills
a couple of decrepit foreign cars parked
on cobblestones
half forgotten images and smells
hiding in shadows on
winding staircases.
Close the wooden doors leading to the cellar
containing life half forgotten half re-emerging.
On the walk to Kalvarijos market overheard
a conversation in Lithuanian:
Zydai dabar yra madingi
Jews are in fashion now.

Anna Halberstadt

THE SECRET GARDEN

is right in the center
of the medieval
half pretty - half demolished
Baroque and Gothic city
old walls covered by graffiti.
Ruins of my childhood
bombed out walls with glassless windows
have been replaced by post-communist
shabby-chic. Volvos
parked in neglected courtyards
broken glass on the grass
mixed with beer cans and
German condoms.
The orchard behind my school
with fragrant red currant and gooseberry bushes
that used to be tended
by nuns in civilian clothing
is gone
but a path
behind piles of construction materials,
as you pass an enormous parking lot
which used to be a basketball court
in the school yard
leads to a patch of the overgrown garden
with craggy apple trees
thistles and weeds,
facing the pink meringue
of St. Katrina's Baroque on one side

and a windowless building on the other
like a skull
blindly staring you in the eyes.
A few minutes away
on Strashuno
now Zemaitiyos street
where my childless aunt Alta lived
her six year old Sara shot in the ghetto
nothing seems to have changed
except for a few foreign cars
parked between decrepit wooden
storage sheds with rusting locks
pots with chamomile and geranium
and a couple of lazily stretching cats.
Old screeching wooden staircase
that leads to the second floor
aunt Alta's apartment doors
little dark kitchen
steeped in the smells
of Jewish cooking.
Chicken soup with home made
egg noodles that I hated
and poppy seed cake
that I loved.
In the bedroom
a folding mirror with a small table
on it
a painted china figurine of a gymnast

thick glass Art Nouveau bottles
a box with old buttons and broaches.
My six year old cousin Grishka
her favorite
because I knew she liked little boys
better than girls
making lots of noise and
breaking her favorite vase.
Last time I had seen her in Israel
a tiny old woman
who cried when she saw me in 1992
standing in front of an old wooden house
in an orange grove in Nataniya.
There used to be an Army and Navy store
around the corner, on Pylimo,
right across from the yellow house where I grew up
now some type of office
with cars parked on what used to be
a little grassy field.
The small park on the left is there
the old bathhouse is now half demolished
half eaten by another building.
The food market
is still a food market,
but looks a great deal smaller
than it looked when I was five.
I am turning back to the ghetto
with plaques on the walls simply stating
how many Jews had been rounded up
and shot right there

or taken to Ponary to be executed.
Vilnius, my Vilne,
my innocent Catholic bride
in a white lace and taffeta
shimmering dress
with a blood stained slip
held by rusted pins
peering from underneath.

Jill Hoffman, "Garter," 2014. Oil on canvas, 40" x 30"

Anna Halberstadt

GOD, GOTTENIU,

I had never been taught the formal language of prayers
I can only talk to you in the voice
of a scared rabbit hiding in the bush
with his stupid little tail sticking out
I can talk to you in the voice of mama raccoon
carrying her striped offspring one by one
by the skin of their necks
away from the two screaming women
that had discovered her nest
in their country house shed.
I can pray to you like a drying out tree
stretching naked branches at night
into the tangerine sky
like the tide lapping against the side
of the wooden pier
in the moonlit sea.
In the yellowed photo ten Jewish women
half naked
clutching each other in anguish
standing with their backs to the pit
ready to be shot
photographed by some unknown executioner
in Ponary
where were you then, God,
you bastard?
I wish I believed that people are good at heart
like the fifteen year old Anne Frank.
I am a little Soviet pioneer in a red tie

saluting you.
I do believe, though, in
the synergy of a beehive,
complex behaviors of ants in an anthill
divine architecture of beaver dams
before a mad hunter shoots the female
and the male begins madly swimming in circles
mourning his mate in the bloody pond.

Vitaly Komar, "Rainbow at the Jewish Cemetary" after Jacob Ruysdael, 2010. Mixed media, 40" x 30"

Steve Haskin
MY FATHER

I remember my father.
I was a small boy standing before the furnace
door as it opened.
He was the blast of scorching heat,
a sand storm through lace curtains,
a nail through the sole of my boot.

I wanted a father who could say
"faith" or "love" or "mercy".
Instead he was like a thousand steps
through the frozen valley of the night.
Birds frozen to the wires.
Zenith slipping from the sky.
Vanishing point vanishing.

"There are men who talk to God,"
someone said.
"Open your mouth, already a mistake,"
my father said.

Nitzan Blouin
TODAY

they found my body
broken in seven pieces,
on Doyers street.
It's a street that is
accustomed to
murder.

The police are still debating whether I
was pushed,
or fell,
or jumped
into a pink night of
rotting Chinatown
midsummer,
New York.

The gray blue of my sleeves
and fading black of my pants
blended into the sidewalk.
Uninterested pigeons
toed
around my strewn curls
picking at stale dim sum.

The fingers of my right hand were
set under the weight of my torso.
It's the mudra of fearlessness,
my Buddhist lama explained,

Index finger touching thumb,
middle, ring and pinky straight.
His Tibetan choked
under the burden
of tears he kept to himself —

like the special prayers
that were reserved for
those who died
under more predictable circumstances.

On the inside of my wrist,
in bright new black
were the letters of your name.

My body was heavier
after I died.
The hazel color of my eyes muted quickly.
My wrists and ankles were
covered with mosquito bites.
The lama said
I had good blood.

The stains disappeared into the pavement.
And by lunchtime,
the pigeons were gone too.

Nitzan Blouin

MR. FARGO

You were late to pick me up at the airport.
My sunglasses didn't cover enough
of my face.

You tried to hide me in the big house
under the painting of the blue flowers.
I danced in the checkered black and white kitchen
alone.

Then we went to the show you curated,
with Tim's urn greeting us,
instead of him standing,
black turtleneck, drink in hand,
dying of cancer by the minute.
His sister was there too.

She told me about her daughter, day trips to the Frick museum
and how to make pastrami sandwiches.
You were selling paintings,
doing bad math in that tall head of yours.

A small band in suits played music.
Nobody understood my foreign accent
and you asked me not
to cuss so much.
I noted your lack of loyalty.

The snow was hitting hard

on the way back to Fargo.
I thought that if I died at least I'd be well dressed.

The gray flakes made
piles of sharp little nails
on the road
We had to stop the car
because your windshield was broken.
I was considering my last words.

The next morning your phone rang
we found out that the rest of Tim's family died
on the way to his own funeral.
They took the same road as we did.

You cried.
It was the third time I saw you cry
and I had known you six weeks.
I held your 6'4" body in my spaghetti arms.
Then you were talking on the phone
to other girls who were crying too.
Most of them liked bacon,
some of them liked you.

I got on a flight back to New York
the next morning.
I haven't been that cold since.

Nitzan Blouin

ADVICE (TO LAURA)

Don't go to Poughkeepsie.
Empty tracks covered with baby green grass,
Rusting stoplights in the middle of the forest,
And a locked train car with decaying white walls.

There are empty benches inscribed with cursive letters,
of orphaned girl scout cookies.
The earth grows daisies and irises.
Your shoes will be stained with mud,
Or you'll end up dead on the floor,

One Wednesday afternoon.
From a heart attack
at the age of 35.
Your adopted baby
crawling nearby
chewing on your shoelaces,
dust bunnies and a blue plastic spoon.
The phone will go on ringing,
you will never pick it up.

Don't go to Poughkeepsie alone, Laura.
You may end up being swept by the winds,
following the beaten path
of the Half Moon on the Hudson River.

Craig Cotter

I'M GAY

but have had
more sex

with women
than most

straight guys

giving it

the college try

Jill Hoffman,"Cupid and The Wolf,"2012. Oil on canvas, 12" x 16"

Steve Mearns

ABSURD

He hanged himself
in that dress
with those red shoes.
How the boys laughed,
and the mothers?
They eyed the shoes.

Charlene Fix

PLUMS WITH ASIAN PEARS

for Linda Carey

If I could, I'd paint these Asian pears in a blue bowl
as if intercepted as they fell, crisp and sudden, from the tree.

And I'd scatter these small plums, gleanings from the same orchard,
near the bowl on the nicked wooden table

until, grown weary of the way the blues compete,
I'd find another bowl and in it let them mingle,

plums with Asian pears, for I like the mix of purple
and chartreuse as I like the smell of dry leaf and sparrow

together for their brief hour. My plums are smaller
than the ones you painted in their shroud of dust

exactly as you found them on your steps the summer before
Charles died. Then you gave me the painting,

plums that close around the evening like soft blue hands.
They rolled to one side of the steps as if to let you pass

while they remained: always now, always right before,
dense and sistered by leaves.

Charlene Fix

COUNTRY AND COUNTRY
for Eric

We were taking lots of rides beyond the city then,
past grounded clouds gauzing a heaven of hazy colts

and mares and meditative cows, and even the occasional
deer grazing wild among them. But you grew confused

when we called this *country*, for you had learned in school
that many *countries* make the world, and yours was America.

How we labored to explain the fullness of the word,
but you folded your six-years' length of arms across your heart,

dismissing us with a skeptical drift of cobalt blue eyes.
You live now way beyond the clouds, in another country

where, at last, we'll all set down our valises full of abstractions
and, like immigrants, take a good look around.

Some will expect winding streets, cafes, and dogs
napping two by two in squares. May they find them.

Others will seek fields of flax and oats, and animals
no hand will ever mar *davening* in fields near open roads,

where deep magenta ironweed shares slopes with orange lilies.

John Gosslee
DISCONNECT

a hot nude
is white wash

a goddess could say
I will worship you

and I would replay
why

everything feels
like a parrot's game

a dance
written for paraplegics

Carlos Fragoso, "Split," Oil, acrylic and charcoal on paper, 52" x 42"

Peter Layton

GLANCES

I'm doing life.

And you got the other.

Our lives once blurred together.
There were two moons in the sky.
Two suns.
Earth extinction meteors
churned through known clouds, I
can't, cannot, the blowing of breath

Seems I remember the dinosaurs
in between thick rubbery leaves
did we wander among them, never looking up

The moons I kind of despise, swim all over me now
your unneeded clothing hangs without speaking
the days all have gathered lonely as ducks and are strange
if I'm caught somewhere when your favorite music shocks from a radio

Margaret Gilbert

TURKEY IN THE STRAW
from SUGARING OFF:

1

Sir Rudolf happened to call The New York City Opera, where I worked, and I answered the phone. I felt like I had found an old friend and promptly suggested that we meet again. He invited me to lunch on Saturday at Harry Cipriani, and I asked him to pick me up at my apartment. It was Tuesday, and I was so excited, the rest of the week was unbearable. I waited for the days to pass one by one until Saturday.

2

My wardrobe trunk had finally arrived from New Orleans, and now I had a Duncan Phyfe chair and a blue wardrobe trunk with gold trim in my apartment, but still no bed. The trunk opened into a small bureau and had drawers and hangers for clothes, but I was still without clothes to put in it. At the opera, Editorial Assistants who earned $8,000 a year managed to wear Halston and Gucci. They got manicures at Kenneth's and rented summer vacation houses in the Hamptons. Many of them lived in doorman buildings where their parents helped pay the rent. I was jealous because I had so little. When my mother sent me another check for $300, I decided to go shopping for a blouse for my lunch date on Saturday. I found a polka-dot see-through chiffon blouse at Hermes for $275 and bought it. It was a stunning blouse even though you could see through it. It really didn't matter what I wore with it.

3

This is the blouse I was wearing when Sir Rudolf came to call in my basement apartment on Saturday afternoon before lunch. I poured him a cup of tea and made him sit in the Duncan Phyfe chair decorated with bronzed sphinx heads. Things became very strained. First, he asked me if I had any boyfriends, and then he groped me. Before I knew it, we were both on the floor of my apartment. Then he stood me up in front of the closet, and kissed me, massaging my breasts through the see-through chiffon blouse. Afterwards, we left for Harry Cipriani, a restaurant in the Sherry Netherland Hotel.

4

I had been shocked by Sir Rudolf's behavior, but Harry Cipriani in the Sherry Netherland made up for it. Harry Cipriani was the first restaurant I had ever eaten in, with chandeliers and pink walls and plenty of daylight from the windows that looked onto Fifth Avenue. The tables all had white tablecloths with gleaming silverware, and the waiters wore white uniforms. We drank champagne. Then we sat at a table in the back where I remembered I was scheduled to work at The New York City Opera that afternoon. Sir Rudolf asked for a telephone, and the Maitre D' brought a white and gold telephone right to our table. It was then that I called The New York City Opera and informed them I would be late to work because I was at Harry Cipriani having lunch with Sir Rudolf Bing. I arrived several hours later for work, my head full of champagne, and was promptly fired from my job at the Opera.

E.J. Evans
LIVING ALONE

This is the last place. The house
is on the edge of the woods.
All the windows open and the wind
blowing through. There's the trail
that zigzags down the hillside
and farther down meets the meandering creek.
With damselflies and goldenrod.
With hawks crying out in the sky,
from their long high spirals.
Sharon said they are messengers of Spirit.
Every day I listen, listen. I hear them,
but I can never remember
what they have told me.

E.J. Evans

WEST WINDOW

Down in the heart it is always autumn.
Always the row of pines
with their branches churning the wind,
and gusts full of leaves swirling past.
The clouds thinning out and the sky steel blue.
The light pouring down again across the lawn.
Late afternoons I watch it thicken and deepen.
You live there on the other hill.
When we are together
the long conversation continues.

Farrell Brickhouse, "Young Sisyphus," 2014.
Pencil and paint on paper, 4 5/8" x 6 3/4"

Marina Rubin
THE JEWISH HUSBAND

her mother always told her: marry a jewish man, little Oksanka, they make the best husbands, they bring all the money home and never beat up on their wives. her father was a baggage-handler at the airport who squandered his miniscule earnings on vodka and when that ran out he drank his wife's perfume, acetone, peroxide. so it was only natural when she grew up, she tucked away her golden crucifix, abandoned easter eggs and mistletoes and started looking for a husband at the local shuls, the jewish centers, the yiddish matchmakers. she found him one day, balding, overweight, uncircumcised, who loved bacon in the morning. she climbed mountains for his affection, immersed in mikvah, took conversion classes, entertained his infinite mishpokhe. they were planning an illustrious wedding when suddenly his uncle died, the wedding had to be postponed according to the jewish law. Oksanka's desperate cry echoed in the halls of the old temple: i don't give a shit how many more of your fucking relatives die, i am still getting married, damn it

Marina Rubim

ZELËNKA

i was just as blond and blue-eyed as the other Ukrainian girls who wore little brass Jesuses on their necks and traveled to grandmothers in villages and fed roosters in wooden coops. one day a doctor came to our house, Dr. Krik, his last name meant scream in translation. my older brother, a boy of fifteen, recently released from the hospital, was in the living room, sprawled out on the couch wearing loose boxer shorts, sighing and moaning. if i peeked at just the right angle i could see layers of skin, hair and bone, covered in zelënka. the doctor assured everything was healing properly. standing in the sunlight like Moses he said congratulations, young man, you are now a real Jew. with my feet barely reaching the floor, i thought so that's what it means to be a real Jew – zelënka in your underpants, and if my brother was a Jew there was at least a 50% chance that my parents were Jews, and therefore i was 25% Jew. i screamed at my parents, how could you, why didn't you tell me, why were you hiding this from me? they said oh, we knew you'd find out soon enough.

zelënka: antiseptic green dye used to prevent infection

Dave Torneo

GREENFIELD

It's 1977,
a late night open mic
at Baudelaire's Café
a year or so
before it shut down for good,
the audience full of punks
and last wave folkies
giving each other the finger,
and he shuffles in, a longer,
prematurely stooped
under a *Weltschmertz* cloak,
wearing the thin chin whiskers
of a derelict Christ.
Rumor had it
he spent time in Camarillo State Hospital,
where Charlie Parker
was detained, drawn and quartered.
But Greenfield had better luck
and came out the other side,
poems like dusty moths
flying out of his rackety Remington.
We would croak
our own half-baked poems
knowing they were fakes,
then Greenfield would
make his way on stage,
his hands trembling,
a little drunk

as he spit his poems at us,
each word
bitter on his tongue.
Maybe his poems
would slowly poison him,
but they were his poems,
even if he were only telling
this crowd of know-it-alls
and street kids
that he was an almost recovered junky
about to fall off the cliff
for the last time.
None of us
would have a drink with him
or invite him to our makeshift apartments,
our converted garages,
smelling of gasoline.
We were too squeamish, untested.
We hadn't lived enough
to know a certain kind of life
can kick your ass
all over the room.

Almost thirty years later
far from loved ones
in an ammonia scented hotel room,
mold in the bathroom,
four heavy locks
on the numbered door,
I flip on the TV
to ease my loneliness
and Robert Longfellow Greenfield,

Dave Torneo

professorial and kingly
in corduroy and elbow patches
reads from his schoolboy's
notebook as the camera
zooms in over his shoulder
and gives a close up
of the poem on the page:
three words writ large
with aqua-marine Magic Marker,
HOMER and THE SEA.

Lawrence Applebaum, photo

Wally Swist
LEFT UNSAID

While I am still here I will open the front windows
To allow the late August coolness to enter the room.

I will sit in a chair beside the dining room table
With the maroon tablecloth and celebrate

My gratefulness with a simple breakfast of peanut
Butter and peach preserve on toast, a glass of orange

Juice, and iced coffee. I will look out at the orb
Weaver webs strung out among the dew of the grass;

And watch the garter snake, that has grown so much
Since last summer, and who lives under the side porch,

Sun on the bricks of the walk. While I am still here,
I will walk in the morning sunlight, and experience

Myself as one with all, as I look out over
The Pelham Hills, still blanketed with remnant wisps

Of vestigial mist. I will accept that which is within
Myself, and come to terms with my having nursed

The urge of hanging a rope up in the barn
And stepping off a chair. For reasons left unsaid,

I will make use of the day every way I can,
While I am still here.

Vicki Mandell-King

FAMILY REUNION
– *Kolimbithre Beach, Paros 2010*

The Aegean blues and beckons.
My son is reading a Stegner novel off my home shelf,

his lover basks in the Greek sun, my husband dozes.
They are here with me in the place I have dreamed of

ever since I first read the glorified stories
of Alexander the Great – his life and conquests –

stories that blurred in a child's eye
with those mother told of my dead father –

a hero in his own world and time, treating the wounded
in war and in the slums, speaking their language.

I decide to swim to the buoy. At first it seems not far,
though distance is inclined to unfurl. Destination

reached, slowly I make my way back – on a slant,
compensating for a strong, off-coursing current.

At least one blue eye has kept watch –
old enough to know how

life succumbs to sudden shifts, its wave-nature
– arch and spill, roll and frill,

and in-between, the lovely lulling interludes.

As I emerge, a casual *Have a good swim?*

Moments later, turning a page, he finds
a folded piece of paper, a prescription

written in 1995 *for Roberta*, my mother
– dead soon after –

who cared not a wit for travel, but would go anywhere
to be with us.

Farrell Brickhouse, "Moving Wood," 2014.
Pencil and paint on paper, 5 3/4" x 6 3/4"

Vicki Mandell-King

DROUGHT'S END

Last night I woke
to a strange sound –

rain

falling through lead sky,
cold like bullets
firing wet.

This morning – life's insistence
in the stiff will
of a new blade of grass

with never a thought
of dry suicide.

Martin Ott

THINGS I'VE LEFT BEHIND

An M-16 carbine, oiled and passed to the next grunt,
muscle memory such that years later I could still
disassemble in the dark more easily than unhooking
a bra. A plastic bucket of Army men in my mother's
attic, plastic edges worn from hardwood missions,
mixed with cowboys, Indians, strange battles looming.
8 mm footage from my college kung fu epic, filmed
in Russian. A '69 Chevelle abandoned five miles
from the airport, bayonet and peyote tossed into brush.
My dog tags dangle on the bedpost of a woman
who led me into former Yugoslavia. The necktie
from my first formal dance flung to lariat a falling
star, my best friend plummeting from Jack Daniels.
The ear clip from those lost years in New Orleans
among men in trench coats and women in Egyptian
jewelry. The bag of pot I buried at the Canadian
border with Woody, the felled hair, skin window
to sun, rain, pitiless drones strafing battlefields
won and lost. Anger, pride, these things take
longer, flotsam of fights with women, tests
with men, so much pain and glory over days
that broke skin, hearts and bridges. On this path
still half traveled, I keep fused bones, shadow
seeds, love of children in a place that even
strangers can see, these steps, this passage of me.

Clay Waters
WHEN I WENT BACK

I did not detour
down the tree-dusked street
with the lemon ice-box house,
that cool, unwitting container.

I didn't picture your upstairs bedroom
or the dark sour den
shared in fierce coeval friction
with a divorced mother,

did not read again those first letters
from under a discreet payphone

did not check if violet still held
to those old envelopes

didn't close my eyes
to listen for thunder striking
from the grassy patch
off the frontage road.

Now we share a city ten-thousand rooftops deep,
a thousand places we'll never meet;
a chopped skyscape
unclumped with accretions
of memories
stamped still in the orange bricks
of a vanished boutique,

coded in the minor keys
of a summer soundtrack
forever infected

and after everything in that old town
is pulled down
still I could trace
the short way to your house
like found gold on a glowing morning
your green-eyed absence
blinking in and out beside me,
only half asleep.

Jim Kerbaugh

THOSE OKLAHOMA HILLS

Gasping heat, grass sunglasses-yellow-brown,
Turd-colored streams,
Snakes, ticks, evangelists.
Ghastly place, gut protruding
Well beyond the belt.
Prayer breakfasts, Jesus
(Native Southern Baptist son)
Tucking into sausage, grits;
Witless witnessing, grease-gravy belch.
Fish-hook in the mouth devotion,
A place to fish for anything but men.
Gun, Bible, tackle, crucial gear:
Better to start than finish here.

Leonore Hildebrandt

THE MEATPACKER'S CHILD

The prince of meat keeps his lot
chock-full of steaming cattle. All day
he summons to his steel-clad hall
their heads, hides, rumps, and hoofs.

I've discovered a secret—
the royal meatpackers bear the names
Knocker, Sticker, Gutter…

They bear these names
bravely, even as the line
disassembles
a bit further each day
and a chill hangs over the stalls.

They shiver in their clothes
at night when the moon calf
bellows to the lost herds.

Morning comes—a shift in the sky—
and the ten thousand heads
turn back and fade.

We are serving a great prince.
Each night, I creep to the window
to count and tally. Mother says,
"Hush, child—don't you know
the blade that rocks the cradle."

Robert Cooperman
MAKING DELIVERIES WITH HARRY: CITY HAT FRAME, THE LOWER EAST SIDE OF MANHATTAN

When Santiago, the delivery man,
didn't show up, Harry—
my dad's partner—drove orders
to customers; I rode wary shotgun:
Harry a fast-handed drunk.

"You think I'm a real prick,"
he demanded, weaving through
traffic like a manic sewing needle.
My mouth dry as a Texas drought:
Harry had slapped me for miscounting
one order of hat frames.

"You're right, kid," he nodded,
"I am a nasty son of a bitch,"
and tilted back his pint bottle.
"But I was an orphan, and before that
my old man beat the crap outta me,
him an even bigger drunk,
and Doberman vicious."

At fourteen, I knew this was as close
as I'd get to an apology, so I nodded.

That night, I asked Dad about Harry.

"He slapped you." Not a question,
and I said nothing, my mouth drier
than in the van, knowing I was a snitch,
knowing Harry was in for the pounding
his father should've given him years ago,
and knowing that was somehow my job.

Max Yawney, "5-25-14," 2014. Two Inkjet prints, 30" x 40" and 16" x 20"

John Randolph Carter
I'M A MACHINE

The polka-dot Bartholomew cries openly.
There's just a whiff of incense.
No one's watching.
Hold your leg and whisper, "No."

Usury is compulsory.
Complain again and again and again.
Before the dominos begin to fall, I'm getting out of here.

The garden is rife with hot sprinklers.
I'm more timid than a torpedo.
Relax. I'm throwing my sombrero.

Your supper's ready.
Will you please forgive the lettuce?
Crab apples will kill you and feel nothing.

John Randolph Carter

BEFORE IT'S TOO LATE, SAMPLE VICTORY

The forest was caked with icing.
My heart was lost in rumpled sheets.
There were vague batteries before the cushion wars.
Lax buttermilk was not human.
Forgotten moss farmers descended the steps of *Catch-As-Catch-Can*.
Before long they thumped the tub, loudly.
Out came pickets with drawn swords.
I was afraid to watch.
Soon there were horseless carriages scattered about the battlefield.
I took pictures, so I could remember.
This was a time of opulence and hocus-pocus.
There were milkmaids on every corner.
I like milk.

Lee Slonimsky
SEETHE

In my most desolate moments,
Harvey Shapiro's poems console me.

But not quite as much as the sunlight
on the red tiled roof
across the street,
ancient as a spider's web,
modern as the bluish glare
of a TV through a window
that sunlight blurs to ghostliness
despite the seethe of noon

Laura Hetzel, "Kaj at the window," 2014. Photo

Zachary Rosen
THE PIANO'S STILL SITTING THERE OUT OF TUNE

The night grandpa died, my grandmother
carved funeral dirges into the keys of their old piano with her fingertips.

There is no music written in the key of heartbreak like that,

so at the funeral they laid him back down into the mud
he'd come from, playing all the blues and boogie-woogie records
he'd kept around the house. Two months later,

I walked into the smell of the home they'd lived in my entire childhood
and found my grandmother there,
pounding her fists on the old piano, naked,
hoping that if he heard her howling the blues he'd loved, like the Wolf in the record
      player,
maybe he'd come back to bed with her,

the wooden hammers snapping all the strings inside the old Baldwin,
and her singing until all that was left was the last breath in the word lonely.

Zachary Rosen

I WALKED OUT OF YOUR ROOM, MY TIPTOES INTACT

Walk out of this room, 'round the corner,
twenty steps in either direction,

I was born there, crying and naked,
same as you was.

Every morning I wake up
and roll out of my blankets, going west.

Some days I tie my shoes on upside down:
I'm tiptoeing on my own sole.

I want to know how
an unpaved road feels like.

Joseph Voth
BARCELONA

Day after day, the city passes
Its time and,
      So you might know things
As they are,
         A woman pours oil
The contour of pearls
        Upon a red leaf.
The marketplace blazes
        Near a pier at the
Water's skin and you stand
        At its edge
With your tongue
In the tumbler of a latch
        And quiet
Your mind to the sea as it
        Is, as it
Will be, unlocking the day,
        Red leaf,
Tide and tongue.

Dear _____ ,

By now, you understand

      We are each a poison the

Other has taken for too long.

The significance of that—"too

long"—is the story of us:

How we searched that great

City in darkness until, from

The garden on a hill, snakes

Reigned in the moonlight

Of our sadness.

Peggy Garrison
HAUL

We were sitting across from each other
doing homework
in the college cafeteria—
he introduced himself—
Ari, from Jaffa.

It was brief
ache-between-your-legs love—
once on my roof—
once in the bedroom of my
playwright friend, Laura.
I remember his smooth back
and slightly hunched-over shoulders—
though still young he resembled
an old Torah scholar.

It's been 20 years—
I guess he's back in Israel,
my friend dead, 15 years—
and the door to my roof
is locked (a matter of security)—

time's haul—I wonder if he remembers
the street-fair he called a carnival
my pushed up skirt.

Peggy Garrison

SET SAIL

Her genitalia
will soon set sail
you don't need a map
to lap her lap

But don't neglect
her little hole
a pencil instead
of a pole.

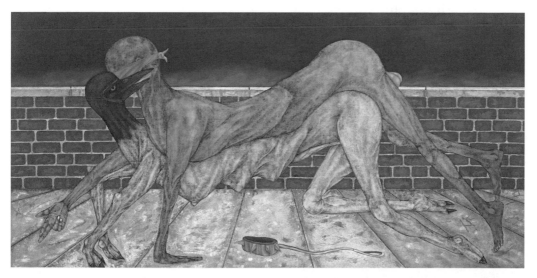

Carlos Fragoso, "Rooftop Games," Oil, acrylic and charcoal on canvas, 112" x 55"

Michael Skau
THE OLD POETS

PICKUP

I've never finished anything—
simply fragments, nothing
I'd want to court, much
less to marry, a life
of writing one-night stands.

MUSES

I cannot write in happiness—
it's just that nothing comes.
Thank God that in this life
I found ample opportunities
for poetry. Give me an insult,
an injury, an infidelity,
the death of one I should have loved,
and watch me masturbate my sorrow.

CRAMMING

My poems are notes
I've taken on life
because I fear God
gives exams the first
day of death.

FOOLS

I've never cared
to make my poems
clear to every
fool who reads
them. Poetry
should be a lover
not a whore.

David Potter, "Coney Island," photo

George Rawlins
WERE

The past is always quiet
A flooding river
With its wonderful junk
Single in its purpose
To put things where
They already are
The place where horses die
Trying to stay beautiful
Where the people we loved
Live without faces
The place where churches
Burn in soundless prayers
Where lovely instinct
Wells up one last time
Moving the moment
Always out of reach
Always falling back

Becky Kennedy

WALKING IN THE SQUARE

Walking out in Harvard Square
at evening when winter's snowing
the air and you're dead
and the snow falls in welts and it's

white, indifferently
on the snow-burdened Charles
and the frozen sycamores.
When you ran once in the square

on a winter afternoon
in a red scarf, your shadow passed
enormously across the snowy
walk and vanished.

And then rebounded, bright
as iron, even brightening
although the limousine of night had pulled in
under the raw boulevard lights.

Becky Kennedy

IT WAS THE END OF WINTER

It was the end of winter, the light returning
to work against the snow stains; you were cleaning
garden trash when the phone rang but it was not
your phone but the cell phone of a roofer across the way;

"Not you again," he seemed to say to the phone;
you were back in the dead leaves. "And using
the kids against me. I know that trick
and your sisters; I know every one of their dirty ways."

You saw where he stood against the sky talking
to the phone cradled at his neck; he was soft
with it; he dangled a hammer and around him
was a buzz of electrical tools; you too were

conversing with one not there, with one no longer
there but present always; you too had your job
with the clay of dead leaves, black moss, the sticks, the rocks,
the stones, so much to say, so much work to do.

John J. Trause

THE MERMAID

.

I

I sing of Viking boats and manatees,
dugongs and diphthongs, faeces,
beautiful brown blooms born of a bellyache,
blubber, spermaceti, ambergris,
whalebone, narwhale spikes, and cuttlepiss,
of cabbages and kings...

II

I sing of hurricanes
/   / / /
/   / /   /
 /   /   /   /
  /   /
      /
  /

III

I sing of cicadas by day,
by night crickets, of chiasmus
and aposiopesis—

IV

I sing of cicada shells
and shells of sea things,
of absence and remnants, of drift,
of less and more, when less is less
more and more and always less than.
I sing of that which neither fish nor flesh
at fever pitch *se relâche*...
I sing of the mermaid from her lair
who buoys up the drowning man,
the mermaid who lets her shift slip

Mike Spikes
R.

her
jalapeños,
rattlesnake
meat,
and
marmalade
in
the
morning

Jill Greenberg, "Neither Fish Nor Flesh," 2006. Plastic packaging
from cosmetics and plastic swimsuit display form

Mike Spikes

TANKA

Wine. Soft music.
Lights low.
April through the window screen.
She takes off
her Ph.D.

Jill Hoffman, "Jean Seberg," 2013. Oil on canvas, 16" x 20"

Mike Spikes

S.

nailed
to the cross
between her breasts

wildflowers
in a cut crystal vase –
nothing but lace panties

talking
dirty to her –
tonight the moon's a Florida orange

Mike Spikes

DON'T APPRECIATE YOUR YOUTH

Don't appreciate your youth.
Want to be
in the glorious future.
Wish you were someone
else
far better.
When you look in the mirror,
assume your face
will never line.
Take your flat stomach for granted.
Believe you can do it
all night long
forever.
Be smug.
Oblivious.
Dream your life away.
You're only young once.
Don't waste it.

Daniel J. Langton

IN THE MIDST OF LIFE

Watching the man cut the fish. He has done
fish as a boy, as a lover, as a man,
he knows to concentrate, he knows his skill
won't make the knife alert, it's up to him.
I watch him slice as I slice bread the sun
is breaking ground, will do what it can.
I can't but think: was he there for the kill,
for that last pull? Did he see the eye die?

I remember the time a Labrador
took on a highway with a look of dread
as real and clinging as a bloodied shirt.
He knew what to expect, and what is more,
when he was driven he was more than dead
as, seeing clearly, we are more than hurt.

Stephanie Emily Dickinson
FIREFLIES

When Florence turned ninety-seven it was time to move into a smaller apartment in the same retirement complex from Village Place up the hill to Village Ridge. Going up the hill meant her rent doubling because nurses would come twice a day to give medication, and since her new apartment had a microwave and no stove, she would eat three meals a day in the cafeteria. Her electric space heater with its glowing orange coils, a fixture in her every bathroom and a comfort all the winter mornings before her teaching days began, would be carted off to storage. "My little heater. I'll really miss it," she kept saying. Village Ridge, divided by a parking lot from Village Place and owned by an Omaha corporation, was the death house. You moved there after you could no longer be trusted to remember your own name. The demon Alzheimer roamed its halls.

"Mom, you can't take all these lids into your new apartment," my brothers said. "There's no room."

"These things are my life," she'd cried out in protest at any of her possessions being discarded, i.e. the thousands of plastic containers, the threadbare towels, the costume jewelry and clip-on earrings. "You people will throw everything away. In my day children divided up their folks' things." It is a very different day— a disposable one and nothing is sacred. Her cupboards were still stocked with the gone foods of my childhood: Jeno's pizza, rock hard Jiffy biscuit mix, melted Tang and Ovaltine, crumbling Me Too graham crackers, wax paper.

"Mom, only what's absolutely necessary moves with you," Joel said. "Nothing that isn't mission-imperative."

"Nerts!" she stamped her foot. "You people."

My brothers made secret trips to the dumpster, throwing out forty garbage bags of margarine containers, cottage cheese containers, oleo and yogurt tubs still bearing the indecipherable names of brands long disappeared from store shelves. Detritus, things in pieces, remnants. My father's watch. The rose glass candy dish with its lid missing. Screws that fit nowhere, skeleton keys to doors in torn down houses. In my mother's day billions fewer people walked the planet's surface; her kind saved everything— they were pleasure-misers in an age where self-abnegation was a virtue. They shopped in grocery stores not supermarkets. Watermelons meant it was late June, the black-seeded red flesh ripe for sale gone by August's end. Oranges, a Christmas treat. They said darn not damn, number 2 not shit. Florence never threw anything away, and I watched the things of my childhood age in their own way. Some becoming relics like the tin picnic basket that carried its last picnic to the park in her 98th year.

And now in the white-walled room so unlike the farmhouse where she was born and raised, where I was raised, I sit in the chair beside her bed. The indestructible Florence lies in a blue-checked hospital gown, her mouth agape. Joel told me last night he'd tried to wake her, tried everything and couldn't. Are we watching our mother slowly overdose, and isn't it better being lowered gently deeper into the final coma? I think of her panic. "There were times last month when she was wailing, her eyes looking off into some horrible place," Joel had said. "Once Brett was trying to read the Bible to her and she told him to stop, 'Go read it to your mother.' And Brett said, 'You are my mother.' There was the time she was getting ready for bed and started to undress in front of us. Brett jumped up, 'Oh, God, Mom! No! Oh, my God!' She was out of her mind. Sure, we've seen her angry and stomping around, but this was out of her mind."

We had asked the nurses to increase her dosage of Ativan and morphine, anything to stop her moaning, her lunging up, grabbing the metal side of the bed with both hands, her strong farm girl hands hanging on as if sinking into a cistern, the cold black water snaking around her body. For her to moan in frenzy, "Me a good Christian," one of the grammarian's last sentences, as if in wonderment at the terrors coming at her. Panic. I wondered where was the Great Comforter.

Had the terrors carried her back to childhood? The raw hunger of the Depression, cold sores on her lips and her Bohemia-born grandmother unable to look at her, a big farmer's handkerchief to blow her nose in? Is she walking to country school, then still walking, living with great aunt Anna so she can go to high school? No buses or buggies come for country kids, no rural consolidated school districts. You live with a town relative if you can after 8th grade and there among the sleek-dressed city girls Florence sits, the country bumpkin.

Joel has found a CD player in a sitting room, borrowed it and two tapes of hymns. "Later, kiddo," he says to me, and then he talks to our mother before leaving. "Brett is on the way. He'll be here in an hour. I'm going now to pick him up from the airport." For the second time in a month my middle brother has flown into Cedar Rapids from Dallas. I wonder if Florence will still breathe when Joel gets back.

I pick up my mother's hand and kiss it, wonder who chose the pewter-colored polish on her nails. I kiss her forehead. I say, "Mom, Mom." How much I regret the running away, the hitchhiking, the selfishness of adolescence, and then later the adult I became, a disappointment, never married, never children, no success, only writing that poetry no one reads. What will happen if she dies before Brett, her favorite, arrives? For days she's breathed from her diaphragm, the machine breathing, a function of the primitive brain, and she smells of Moonlight Mile body lotion from Bed, Bath & Beyond that the aides lotion her with. She has never smelled so fruity. Blue Grass was the perfume she wore on her dates. Her skin looks smooth, unwrinkled, decades younger, as if dying is extreme Botox. Soon she'll be newborn.

The aide Ashley pops into the room, her eyes shining, "How's she doing?"

"The same," I say.

"Oh," she says, crestfallen, "do you think Florence would like her nails polished?"

I glance up at Ashley, the one whose pale blue eyes brighten when she approaches my mother with her bucket of polishes. All morning she's been running in and out, standing by when Hospice was here, listening. Ashley, who never learned Botany or Latin, who couldn't teach Algebra or Beginning Reading like my mother, this Ashley, raised on reality TV and her smoke break, wants to be here for Florence's last breath.

"Could you take the polish off her nails?" I ask, knowing Florence would not want the Deeded Body people at the University of Iowa to see that shade.

"Sure," Ashley says, sitting on the bed and placing my mother's hand in her lap.

The window's drapes are drawn and the white room is filled with June sun. I smell the polish remover. Cutex. A familiar odor, reassuring. I wait for the aide to leave, and then I take out her Bible, her devotionals, and put the tape of hymns in the CD player. A hillbilly voice wafts up, singing "In the Garden," and is strangely beautiful. I gather up my mother's photograph albums. Weapons with which to confront death. I start to turn the pages. Maybe it is the Red Cross she loved best, wearing the tailored uniform and poofy bangs and the just-past-the-shoulders Rita Hayworth hair, a recreation worker, a paid position she'd always pointed out. In California and Arizona, wearing the nylons so prized during WWII on her shapely Florence Telecky legs. All the attention from returning servicemen. Snapshot after snapshot. Florence with a man in uniform, his arm round the small of her back. But she remained chaste until her wedding day. Where did those legs come from since her mother and aunt were both thick-ankled? There she is at a formal dinner with other Red Cross nurses, and men in uniform on either side of her, a polished wood table with goblets of tinkling water, one of the men an officer.

I think of Paul McCartney speaking to an interviewer about his first wife Linda's death from breast cancer, and how Linda had entered the coma with McCartney and the children gathered around her bed. And he talked to her, telling her it was a spring day and the bluebells bloomed and she was mounted on her favorite horse and riding into the heather. I lift another of her albums. I want to find a beautiful day to send my mother into.

Here is a photograph of a long ago picnic and there's my father and his parents, there's Uncle Morris with the rotund stomach and Aunt Kate with her upswept hair, so this is a Chicago park. Picnicking, the food you might have eaten at home tastes better and happier in the sun. The green everywhere in the black and white photograph dazzles. I imagine that she will walk into this day where you can see the willow wands floating, leaving their shadows on the picnic table. "Mom, it's a beautiful summer day and we're going on a picnic," I keep saying, "and you're wearing your turquoise dress with the white polka dots, and the strand of white beads." I tell her we're all there. Joel and Brett in their tiny pressed shorts and shirts, their hair parted on the side and holding hands. I'm in a pink dress that matches the ribbons in my fine hair. There's a breeze. Florence has raised her hand to her bangs to keep them from being mussed. Her Rita Hayworth hair has been trimmed, a married woman and mother of three needs shorter hair, but it's still below her ears. My father wears a white short-sleeved shirt of filmy opaque material, and his black hair is trimmed close to his head, his exceptionally large dark brown eyes are reproduced in the faces of his three children. Florence's eyes are a vivid blue. Everyone is relaxing in the willow breeze and I want my mother to believe she is walking back in time where there's smoke rising from the grill, and a frosted layer cake someone has just lifted from a picnic basket. I hold a tin cup. Lemonade. How cold the cup is.

I'm telling her how beautiful she is. Her children are still innocents. And there are the old ones in their humility and kindness.

There's Florence Ruth sitting on the front steps of the farmhouse, her sister Vlasta stands behind with her hands resting on Florence's shoulders. The orchard's in full bloom, throwing black-green leaf shadows into the porch windows, like the two beauties had been created from leaf litter.

More Florence. This time she's twelve years old and being confirmed. The portrait is formal. The boys in the back row stand awkwardly, sons of the farm in homemade haircuts, their suits with puckered seams. The girls sit on a bench. Florence wears a white puff-sleeved dress, stockings and shoes to match, her ladylike ankles crossed. All the girls' dresses are white. All able now to eat the flesh and drink the blood of Christ. They are photographed by the country church in a glade of hickory and oaks. The confirmation class of the dead. My mother is the prettiest of the girls—some are slump-shouldered; others stare at their hands. She holds herself perfectly. Her posture stays with her until the end. A white rose with ferns and stem is pinned to each girls' upper left shoulder. Reverend Porkory, whose theological treatises now live under glass in the Cedar Rapids' Czech Museum, sits in the front row, a rose in his lapel, one hand inside his jacket like Napoleon, his beard not yet the yellowy white you remember from childhood, the brown oval surrounding his mouth where the pipe stem stained it. The tobacco smell of his kiss.

From the CD player comes more of the hillbilly twang. Jesus loves me surrounds the bed. Florence loved to sing in her clear soprano voice. "Daddy was proud of my voice," she'd said. Jesus loves me this I know. Childlike, countrified, beautiful. Something of the music must be getting in or the body itself is responding. I've been watching her for days for a change in expression, noting the eye blink when Rob called and I put the phone to her ear, the one sign of response. Now I hear her machine breathing falter, the primitive brain breaths are softer, the lifting and filling, the falling. The body is relaxing, the music seems to be making that happen. I hit the CD player's stop button. I want Brett to get here. The phone rings and it's Joel and they're pulling up to Village Ridge. Her breath weakening. "Hurry," I say. "She's going."

"Mom, Mom, hold on." I'm sitting on the bed, my hand on hers. "Brett's here. Brett's coming."

Hurry, she is leaving us behind, leaving behind the buttercrank morning when she knocked out her two front teeth, leaving the four stories of the farmhouse, the root cellar's dank where the mysteriousness of sauerkraut happened, the crocks, the handfuls of rock salt crumbled over the shredded cabbages that would sleep for the winter in their cold brine and wake fermented in a different world.

There is a bubbling sound starting in the back of my mother's throat—it's coming, her birth into death, and this life that began in September in another age is ending. I hear Brett in the hall. "Hurry, Brett! Hurry!"

It is all disappearing, the honey and eggs, the windmill, the milk house, riding the black pony, the brother she adored, Luther, the best dancer who truly loved her, Western Dance Hall, the stars, the Depression that taught her every lesson. Hurry, Brett, hurry, she's taking it with her. 3 cents a bushel for oats. Hurry.

My brother runs into the room just as I hear a bubbling sound in her throat like milk beginning to boil. The moment Brett takes her hand the bubbling ceases. Not like the death rattle I've read of, hollow and loud, but soft, like the fizzing of milk left on the stove too long. Nights she could not sleep she warmed milk to sooth her nerves. Brett and I look at each other.

Orphans. Tears spill from his warm brown eyes but he smiles. My brother is a man of light. When I glance over his shoulder I see Ashley a few feet from the bed. Then Joel rushes in. I tell him Mom took her last breath just as Brett walked in. "Mom, took her last breath…she waited for Brett…" Joel who has not cried, begins to sob. He repeats, "Her last breath." Ashley moves closer to the bed. I no longer care. Let her look. The tears I could not stop during the last five days have dried up.

Jill Hoffman, "The Jewish Supremes," 2013. Oil on canvas, 40" x 30"

Charles Cantrell
REFUSALS

for Jonathan Kozol

The hospital near the bay refuses to dispose of used
syringes, old blood, and toxic this and that
properly, puffing its cloudy aftermath
on a school across the water,
which causes half the kids to cough and choke—
asthma. I taught poetry there to 3rd and 4th graders,
watching childhood in action: handkerchiefs
beside pens and paper, baloney between
white bread for lunch—and now and then
a good line or two: *A rose-colored car*
bobbed in the bay for no reason.
Or, *My mother watches Bay Watch and says,*
"I have a better body," then she smokes something
in a pipe and weeps over the Bible.

Mike Faran
TEMPS

After a hideous, week-long stint
in a meatpacking plant,
I was assigned a construction job
in a rented hall in Beverly Hills.

My fellow worker was a sweet
Latino boy named Carlito with
dark brown eyes.
On our lunch-breaks, we shared
sandwiches, coffee – our dreams.

Carlito wanted to be a poet & an actor.
But a poet first.

I wanted to get through life without
falling in love with another man.
But I only told him that I wanted a
shack on the beach.

During our three weeks of backbreaking
labor,
Carlito showed me five poems -
each more beautiful than the other.
They didn't rhyme but, in a sense, they
did.

We shook hands & he was on his way.
I half-followed him for two blocks
through instinct.

Then, from compassion, allowed my
poet to vanish into the long waves of heat
on Sunset Boulevard.

Laura Hetzel, "Beau, Girard Park,"2014. Photo

Mike Faran

PRAY THAT IT'S LOVE

drinking women are the only kind
who can understand me now

they commiserate, relate, empathize ......
all the bullshit words the doctors
use
before the big blue pills

and it's a good feeling to have a
woman hanging onto you
because you can help her up after
she falls flat on her face

you wait hours outside the ER
smoking
often in the rain -
happy as hell to have her back again

even on crutches with a swollen jaw
you take her back to the small room &
sit by the heater with
strong drinks & soft jazz

then she's out

(you can't - goddamn it - drink scotch
after them big blues!)

Mike Faran

but she's up making breakfast in the
morning &
from your dark deathlike sleep
you smell the coffee
hear the bright clatter -

feel her soft kiss & pray that it's love & nothing worse

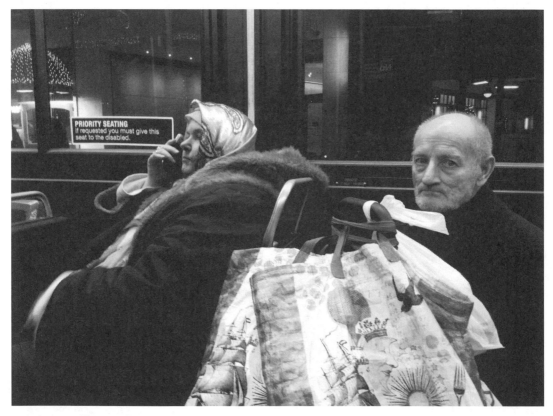

Lawrence Applebaum, photo

Michael Lee Phillips

PAELLA

I spent one summer loading boxcars and flatbed trucks
with fifty kilo sacks of potash, borax, soda ash and pyrobor.
The crew chief was a short guy known as Stump.
An ex-Marine, Stump configured the boxcars we loaded,
calculating the number of bags to be put in each tier,
doing so methodically with a stubby pencil and a scrap
of cardboard. It would take ten minutes of pencil-licking
before he came up with the right configuration. Once,
the third or fourth time we had the same load numbers,
I looked into the boxcar and rattled off the configuration
before Stump could get out his pencil. I'll never forget
the look on his face. Shame won't permit me to describe it.
Instead, let me say this: as soon as I uttered the numbers
but before I could manage the smug, college boy grin,
a guy we called Rat, whose biceps were as big as my
thighs, clubbed me on the side of my hardhat so hard
that it landed twenty feet away in the dirt. I feel no
shame describing his face: It sloped down from two beady,
black eyes past a protruding, wedged-shaped nose down
to a thrusting jaw. In the jaw were teeth that jutted
forward, as if they were eager for more meat.
It was a predator's face, and it looked like it was
coming at you even when he wasn't looking at you.
He didn't need to say anything and he didn't.
He showed me a fist, and I nodded and my ears
didn't stop ringing for two hours and a fierce silence
took over the boxcar as we loaded the bags that

Stump sent out to us. At lunch we sat at our tiny table.
I had a baloney sandwich on white with mayo and Rat
was eating something nobody else could look at and eat.
Stump pulled out a plastic tub from his paper sack.
A modest tub with a lid held on with a thick rubber
band, and under the band was a fork, a fork so polished
it sparkled under the bare bulb above our table. The
handle of the fork was decorated with bits of turquoise,
each little gem as clear and blue as a High Sierra lake.
With that fork Stump would eat his paella, slowly, precisely,
as if he had to configure the space inside his stomach.
Everyone knew that his wife made it from an old
recipe that came over from Spain. As soon as Stump popped
the lid, the tasty aroma would fill the air and Rat would shake
his head trying to hide his smile. On the way to the lunch room
Rat had slapped me on the back of my neck, but playfully.
"Look," he said, "Here it's better to be quiet than to be smart."
At lunch I didn't say a word. I watched Stump eat his paella,
watched how carefully the fork found just the right amount
each time and how careful he was with each mouthful that came
to his lips. When he had finished eating, he washed the fork
in the sink and placed it back on the tub under a rubber band.
This was not a seminar. There were no grand topics awaiting
discussion after we ate. We rested. We were silent, making peace
with our digestion, perhaps. Stump leaned back against
the wall, folded his arms across his chest and appeared to doze.
Rat crossed his arms on the table. Soon, his head dropped
down to his chest and he, too, appeared to be sleeping, yet
his eyes remained open. I sat and listened to their breathing.
Outside our cramped lunch room the old debates continued –
steam venting its rage at the way metal tried to hold it back,

gears screaming for their daily oil, boxcars gripping and
ungripping their massive iron fists, their handshakes crashing down
the line, diesels large and small protesting each clutching gear
change – it was not a bad place to learn the craft of silence,
and I listened as one apprenticed to the loud eloquence of machinery.

Clemens Weiss, "A speech to artists," Stainless steel, writing/ink on glass, transparent glue, 2013.
Diameter ca. 32"

John Paul O'Connor

AS LONG AS I LIKED

When my father came to visit me
in jail, he shook his head and said,
how could you do this to me?

My mother brought me soup.
The police guards said it wasn't allowed
but she nagged them until they relented.

This was her power. I ate the soup
after she left, heard the guards laughing
on the other side of the door.

It was January and a bitter wind broke
through the alley when they let me out.
I hitched a ride to Raymond's house

where he let me sleep on the mattress
in the extra room with no heat.
When Raymond went to work

his wife came into the room
and made love to me on the mattress.
At home my mother cooked me dinner

and said I could stay as long as I liked.
That night a blizzard covered the ground.
In the morning I watched my father

from the upstairs window shoveling
his car out of the driveway.
I knew as soon as he left I would pack

my suitcase and go. My mother
was downstairs humming over the dishes
a melody that would linger for days.

David Potter, "New Zealand," photo

John Paul O'Connor

BILL BAILEY

I never believed in marriage.
She kept pushing me back
and pulling on my necktie.
I caressed her with the passion
of a kissing cousin,
Trish, I think her name was,
though I hesitate to remember for fear

she'll cash in the reward
for my imprisonment.
I'd land behind the bars of matrimony,
where beautiful and smart women
stand guard in watch towers,
cracking glass with their rifle butts.

I wanted the big house on Maple Street.
The boy and girl two years apart,
playing around us while we set the table
with lace made in paradise.
The dog fetching the stick from the pond.
Melodies from the bandstand,
a trombone sliding, *Won't you*
come home, Bill Bailey?

Someday I will. It'll be late summer
and someone will be standing in the yard
hanging out clothes, each cloud racing

to be first on the horizon, and I'll recognize
her standing there with the features
of every woman's face but my mother's.

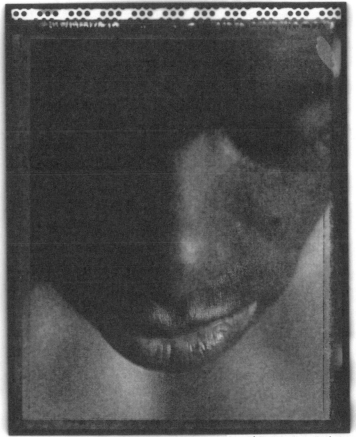

David Potter, "Lee," photo

John Paul O'Connor

POURING DAY

Every Friday our boots are caked with gray,
heavy as the sky. The foreman brings a case
of beer to the bridge and we sit with our legs
dangling toward the river, watching the alder
branches twist dreamily in the current
as we exchange the same scatological and venereal
jokes, scandalizing the entire human race,
ourselves included, and everything we stand for.
It's easy, for there's not much more than this beer,
with its weak taste and strong palliative
and the quest of getting laid on a Friday night.
We're all thinking the same thing; the weekend
and how it leads to Sunday night and the consideration
of Monday. Danny runs his fingers over a two-inch
shred of excess concrete snapped from the end

of a strand of rebar and lets it fall to the water.
Everyone watches as a sudden small wind
pushes it away from its trajectory and into a muddy
pool close to the bank, where inexplicably
it floats and twirls counterclockwise like the hand
of a stopwatch in reverse. The beer runs out
and one by one we crush our aluminum cans
in our fists and rise to walk across our work
to head home. Maybe because we're a little drunk
we reach to touch one another with our open palms,
white with lime, on a shoulder or an arm

or the place in the middle of the back just below
the neck. Or maybe because it's pouring day
and what was laid today will harden and nothing
in this world or any other will change that.

Jack Herz, "Melting Crystal," 2014. Oil on canvas, 24" x 30"

John Grey

TO THE ARGENTINEAN POET

You're sorrowful because no one
cares enough to lock you up these days.
Everybody's too busy hating bankers.
You criticize the government and
may as well call your verse, "so what."

You have the passion, no denying that.
Your first reaction to the hurt, frustrations,
is to get them down on paper.
You're a poet no matter how
the bureaucrats might classify you.

But you're nostalgic for the time that
presidential stooges came for poets in the night.
Years in prison…what a career move.
How better to get your work out there
than to be never heard from again.

It's not that those in power
have thickened up their skins.
It's just you're low down
on the scale of scathing critics.
Jackboots come down on other heads.

What must it have been like
when writers headed up most wanted lists,
when students whispered forbidden names
on campus and, the softer the sound,
the louder the becoming legend,

Now, you read your work
before an audience of three in a coffee house.
In the newspaper, you're listed under local color.
You go for the throat, the patrons nod,
and then everyone retires to watch the soccer.

No troops burst in. No warrants are served.
It's easier to have a book out
than to be shot at dawn.
People ask what you do and you reply. "poet"
and they say, "No, what do you really do."

It's to the point where you'd like nothing more
than to go to the local police station
and give yourself up.
From the list of available crimes,
you could pick the closest one to breathing.

Mimi Zollars

GIVE ME A DARK ROOM AND I WILL GIVE YOU AN ADULTERESS

you are lying in bed
at the other end of the long universe
beside your wife   not touching

I luxuriate
having avoided another maze of sundays
unetched palms of my hands
smooth as the inside of my soul

wild hair unleashed
the dark sea of this room
sybarite curtains glow

I feel your desire
other   lover   familiar

intense complicity
fraught with danger
this potent violet evening

passion seeks its level
in my poets heart
longs to be immortalized

be afraid

Michael Hettich

FIRST LOVE

There was grass growing through the weave in her sweater,
pushing out at her wrists, up over her collar.
She was sitting on a rock that could have been a bench
if the woods had been a garden, and talking to me
about feathers, how they're dreamed in the egg,
how they start out as hollow straws, like hay,
how they turn then to flowers, and finally feather
into feathers; she was talking so softly

I had to lean close, and I saw that the grass
pushing through her clothing was richly green,
like a pelt—not like the tall grass of the meadow
that surrounded us. Her breath smelled like flint or bone,
so I held my own breath. I had wandered off
the familiar trail through the woods where we'd played
hide-and-seek, and where I'd gathered branches
for the darkness. I'd just wanted to explore

by myself for once. There was mica in the stone
she sat on but there were no birds in the trees.
My teeth felt like pebbles in my mouth, and my speech
was garbled when I tried to tell her I was lost,
that I knew now I'd never be found, though I knew
my way home, since I'd paid careful attention
to the trees as I walked, careful attention
to the boulders and the creeks. Let me tell you the truth:

when she took off her sweater and jeans and stood there
before me, I could see her body,
as pale as ivory or the moon, beneath
the lush grass that covered her, that had been ripped
and torn a little when she stripped herself naked.
There were wildflowers too. I was just a boy,
though I knew about yearning. And then she lay down
without a single word. Do you understand me now?
She turned away and lay herself down then as grass.

Jack Herz, "Red Wind,"2013. Oil on canvas, 48" x 36"

Esvie Coemish
LOVE LETTER 23

Autumn Drops Its Head in Its Spaghetti

I can grow entranced with a bread bowl's mush,
imagine your face in each infested flower,
and like a spore latched to prevailing wind
I float, helplessly, toward your body's soft sun.
What a tactless stuntman I've become,
breaking my brain as I leap inside your ink's
scrawl. When I come I come like a leaf blower

spiraling toward the earth. Finished
with stars and the junkyard municipal park,
I count your shoes: twenty-five. Where
there's madness a chain dangles from a fan
that hangs above my bed like an impatiens'
live entrails. Tell me what we can bear.
Tell me the core of the night is a lark's

gizzard cramping the gelatinous
messiah's bones back to stardust,
that it's you speaking to me like a tape recorder's
housefly hum. My soul is not a car,
but I sit in it, wait for help. Carve
my name on the dash: *Esvie was here
or there.* All the time I make a fuss

like a startled rooster. Some nights you tryst

with numbers rushing on the cable box,
my ass depressing the channel button.
The leaves seem to have fallen all at once
to the suffering grass. Usher
the season of dancing, the mud sin,
cracked bites of skin like purple phlox.

Paul Wuensche, "Barnes View," Oil on canvas, 30" x 90"

Robert Levy

AFTERMATH

In memory of P.L.

Compassionless winter scoured the landscape
of all things lush or intimating life
so our hoped-for Spring retreat became a dirge
in mottled brown: scraggly, ruined branches

strewn across the lawn like dead men's bones;
trees with dowager's humps; the deck destroyed
where icicles had plummeted like missiles,
smashing the bird feeder and chaise longue.

The fallow house breathed a funereal hush,
so we slept in, unable to rouse ourselves
for leaden afternoons promising nothing
but combing the lawn for wreckage. We tried

to make a game of it: Who could collect
the most twigs? Stooped low like Millet's gleaners
we were unpaintably sad, gathering
gnarled kindling for fires we could not ignite

within us. *Some vacation*, my wife complained.
Still, there was unlikely liberation
in putting the debris to rest, a strange calm
as after funerals (we'd had our share)

when turning away is also turning towards
what remains—the turbid, mournful keening
of a gray, unthinking wind though tree limbs;
the misplaced explosion of a robin

on the lawn—all of it a reminder
that both the death of seasons and of friends
is as one: reluctant celebration
of a vast and fractured continuance

we must embrace if we are to live with
the brute heaviness of going forward
into each day's night with a soft shining.
So we labored all that bleak March day,

speaking little, dragging ice-scarred tree trunks
to the shed for fitful sawing into logs.
When evening came at last (Thank god for night!)
we went about our disparate duties,

feeding our bodies, putting out the trash,
playing Bach, Mozart until we sickened
from the beauty of it. How could such sounds
fill this arched and timbered space with anything

but death, and how could we not acknowledge
that in this music was a ghostly noise
of tramping feet continuing their rounds
and making sure the house was shut up tight?

That night we made a fire of our achievements
—twigs and branches collected through the day—
and sat silently near the hearth, huddled
in a queer radiance that shed no warmth.

Robert Levy

SHELLING

Full moon inhales the tide tonight, leaving the shore
    breathless with papery lightning whelk egg cases—
        ropy, corkscrewed intestines crackling underfoot

where the gray flats deliquesce to the horizon,
    desert-anonymous, though brimming furtively
        with beached life. I wake my logy son in time

for shelling, when the truly avaricious
    rise in search of junonia, alphabet cones,
        and fragile paper figs. Over calcium wreckage,

with rakes and buckets, we tentatively amass
    the moonlit dead, a mummified palette
        of abandoned mollusk homes, each work of art

with no discernible artisan. By law one can only reclaim
    abandoned domiciles: paired blanched angel wings
        bereft of seraphim, the antlered horse conch

shed of its equine core. My son proudly displays
    a banded tulip which he hoists above the surf
        until, from its whorled den, a slow unfurling

of gelatinous suckered arms slowly reveals
    a baby octopus that's cadged a makeshift home.
        He pokes it with a stick, a boy's questioning.

The cephalopod spurts jet ink and scoots away,
      leaving behind a writhing limb. He pursues it,
            trying vainly to coax it back into its abode.

I killed it, he moans, and flops down on the sand.
      Later we arrange our plunder on the deck,
            calico scallops in a hued panoply

that dazzles the eye with its fecundity.
      My son's lost in thought, curled in his own brittle shell
            of self-recrimination. He has killed today,

and slain, as well, something in himself that cannot
      be reclaimed. Tendriled clouds sweep over the moon's
            baleful eye as he slumps on the edge of the bed

and turns from the shells to look up at the sky
      asking—inconsolably—*Why, Dad,*
            why is it that clouds have tentacles?

Ace Boggess

DREAM GIRL

I look for the woman that walks through the graveyards of raindrops
rather than skirting edges in the street to keep her stockings dry

I look for the woman for whom madness is a candle she waves at night
one to share the swirling cotton strobes she keeps within her

I look for the woman wisely knowing although both bear & caterpillar
lock themselves in private rooms, the grizzly rises up with luminous wings

I look for the woman with eyes gray as the misty beards of mountains
hands so delicate they turned to dust against my cheek

I look for the woman possessed of a secret vault
in which she stores her riches & her dead that came before her

Ace Boggess

THE PARAMETERS

fifteen steps
to cross the cell

from steel wall
to steel wall

ten from cage
to window

enough space
to tango

not enough
to race

five doors
two gates

a hundred fifty
miles home

freedom is luxurious
a haven

heaven
of simplicities

without its own
mathematics

not even
the counting

of hours
or of days

Laura Hetzel, "Cement," photo

Edward Romano
FEAR AND TREMBLING

You might be right in the middle of a girl
or snapping your fingers to a peppy tune
when suddenly the thought occurs
      that someday you must die
          and just like that
             you're all moped out and pouty
to think that after you're gone
the dance goes on without you.
And at that moment it doesn't help
to think that every man must die.
It's only you that matters to yourself.
      But then you think – Ah what the hell
          I'll squeeze some juice from this lemon
            if it kills me.
But for the rest of your life you're never
quite sure what your attitude should be
toward whatever it is that's coming next.

John Hitchens
THIS WINDOW CLOSED

My father arrives home
in early afternoon
as yellow leaves flutter
on the maple in our front yard.
From my high window I watch him—
suit jacket unbuttoned, tie loosened—
stride across the lawn,
the tips of his shoes slicing grass.
I hear my mother slam kitchen cabinets,
snap plates onto the table.
It is fall
when "This Window Closed" marks
his bank teller's station,
and when his black hair silvers at the temples.
Yellow leaves fall early,
lie on the grass like discarded hands.
I turn to radio
where songs sing make-believe stories.
My father paces room to room
window to window.

Susan Cohen

DEATH IN THE FACE

The webbing of her right hand
blackened weeks before,
but I missed the meaning
and walked in on her: skin umber,
teeth clamped as if she worked
at something hard.

I bent from the waist and pecked
her cheek three times
like a mechanical toy bird,
and then I fled. Why?

Legs make up their own minds.

When my legs that wouldn't bend,
then wouldn't stay, took me back
to ask was she still there, I saw her
face like paste, jaw sprung.

In her open mouth, no thirst.

In her face, no recognizable hunger.

My hand, unschooled
in ritual, grabbed hers,
although I barely noticed how

my animal body refused to part
with the body it was part of.

We held hands until I felt no warmth.
Then my mother was a small,
unquestionable corpse.

Carlos Fragoso, "Red State," Oil, acrylic and charcoal on on canvas
36" x 50"

Rob Cook
PORTRAIT OF SOME OTHER SELF

Forty three years of talk
that I've saved,

one bookcase that leans,
one work table that denies

my position among
the long-running goodnight

cast of Lower East Side
make believe,

sunlight approaching
from the readings of Brooklyn,

the close-cropped lady staring with her makeup
while I shop for cage-free eggs,

cage-free bread, free-range
paper towels,

also chocolate that's become
my heart's friend,

watermelons
with the factories removed,

a woman at home better
for me than the Shakespeare dynasties,

better for me than
the scholars of seasons lost,

also an air conditioner
circa 1975, an oven settled

by cockroaches, a toaster
conquered by its crumbs and blackouts,

a photograph taken by L. Applebaum,
a painting by J. Hoffman,

exactly six pencils from
Poe's Cottage and thirteen

pens written dry,
density of polyurethane at 2am

from the downstairs
neighbor

who climbs the fire escape
in hard Russian,

his sheets clanging
between curses of wind

here in the magnolia sightings
of the warmest March,

its car horn clams and headlights
devoured by the East River,

meant only as a rose roof's happiness
and not the wrong wishes to come.

Laura Hetzel, "Jill in her studio," 2013. Photo

Rob Cook

BLUE FINGERNAILS

She answered the door with blue, seconds-long fingernails and a fragrance that smelled like gardenias rotting and sneaking under a missing girl's body upstate in Harriman. Knowing that I could be missing as well, I asked her if I could use the bathroom. She smiled and pointed to a door hanging drunk and rusted from its iron hinges. I examined myself in the slow-thinking mirror: I could still see my face, and I was able to make tiny circles in the air with my tongue. After I finished using the toilet I noticed a used condom dribbling dead milky children along the otherwise fresh tiles. A cactus began to grow in my stomach, my penis fattening for its own slaughter against my dumb-as-always zipper. When I walked out of the bathroom I saw Blue tucking a small girl into cold futon blankets washed with channel 11 half-light. She told me over the Telesex Date Connection that she babysat her neighbor's kid every night from midnight to seven a.m. We went into her bedroom and she handed me a Coors Light. Then a photograph with her in front of the television holding a three-month puppy, the back scrawled: "Dear Robbie, With Love Always, Antoinette from the Line." She tied my long hair into a rope down my back. "You look like some weird god in all this bedsheet darkness," she told me, motioning for me to finish my beer and join her beneath her pink negligee. "I like to touch men with my fingernails," she said, licking them one by one. We kissed until our bodies became deep enough for moistening and the strict emotions of penetration. A light was blinking outside from someone else's search. The phone rang once and returned to where it came from. "You're deep enough to make ten babies," she said more like a photograph than a person. We were sweating in oils and syrup-sticky amaretto, and I heard the little futon girl whimpering through the bedroom door, "Mommy, I'm sick." Blue looked and sounded like her flesh was coming, tattoos of orchids quivering and bludgeoned around her breasts. The lit-

135

tle girl could've been a moth shrieking from a phone booth ten blocks away. She sobbed harder into the door and Blue untangled herself from the hot twisted sheets and put on a lavender bathrobe and disappeared into the next room. The light stopped blinking outside. The phone rang and again died after only one ring. I picked it up and listened to it purring. *Like all the lost fetuses*, I thought. And then I heard Blue say to the little futon girl, "If you keep moving, how will sleep ever find you?" When she returned I was still hard. I was thinking about how many microscopic eyes and lungs must've spilled onto her embroidered pillowcases that week alone. I lied that I missed her while she was gone and again crawled into her.

Konrad Stump
THE RABBITS

I say I love you I love you I love you, and each time I kiss you snot
               gets on my upper lip, but I don't care, I want you
     the way eyelids long to press
   against each other, the way
        fingers are always rubbing. It is winter. You are beau-
tiful.
     Tell me those are tears. Tell me my hands feel like kindling
   and you want to set them on fire. I'll bring the matches, you bring
the story
       of the rabbits, how they were hanging,
    skinned and bloody in the tool shed,
and you took their photographs, you
  let them know that they were lovely,
    that you had never seen a red as deep as kinship.

FISHING MEN

On the surface of the water, your face rippled.
The arms of crabs were breaking it, reaching at us
from their triangular cage. The one we fastened.

The smell was awful, and the light of the moon
gleamed off your teeth as the trap unlatched
into the bin I helped carry.

"This is how we live." Father,

you taught me to snap their legs like snow peas,
to suck the sweet meat from the holes. And their bodies,
useless caverns, we scraped them by platefuls into the trash.

We were famished. We were full. We were famished.
And the taste of the crabs still lingers, like you,
who taught me to relish death so hungrily.

Charmagne Sarco
FROG GIGGING WITH MY FATHER

It was a moonless night, a near storm
breezing them to chorus the end of drought.
We heard them across the tobacco field,
bluegrass bands tuning up. Your gig was trident,
a fourth hook soldered on thumb-wise,
a straightened coat hanger around your waist.

No one would go with you but
Bobby and I caught up to your flashlight
sweeping the sandy path to Dead River.
We had to sit on the bank and be still.
You held the light in your mouth, your face
a glowing red mask, scanning for
the widest pairs of eyeshine,
green and gold Christmas bulbs
caught in what they must have thought
a bedeviling sunrise.

Bobby called the frogs "pooting jugs" and
made fart noises. We laughed so hard.
A swoosh, then things quieted except
your splashing and the colored lights
went out everywhere.

We could smell the rain-pennies and
nickels—because we were half-bloods
raised by black panthers, nested in weeds

at home in the dark, wishing that you were a
friendly monster who would teach us
something to make us famous.

On the way home, we thought we heard
baby birds. "But where are they?" I asked.
You turned the light to your metal hoop
strung with bullfrogs skewered through
the bellies, legs swaying like a hula skirt.

Aunt Mickie screamed and ran inside.
The first lightning bolt split open a noon sky.
Papaw said, "Stay out here Joe,"
while he got you a tub to slide them off into.
"Get me my tin snips," you said to Bobby.

Afterwards you brought the legs inside,
piled high on Mamaw's good platter, hosed off
pink, footless, attached at the pelvic bone.
You handed me a box of salt and said to
sprinkle it or they would not keep.

They began to kick, life still being
so close at hand, trying to swim away
as they had before when the bladed light
came out of nowhere
toward the dark thunder and downpour.

I dropped the box on the floor. You howled
at my slack-jawed silence, my saucer-wide
stare. The ones around the edges
made it off onto the tablecloth where
little Dutch girls clogged around the border,
curtsying the onlooker,
holding up their aprons at the corners.

Jill Hoffman, "Shepherd and the Sheep," 2011. Oil on canvas, 40" x 30"

Charmagne Sarco

THE JUICIEST TIME

We welcomed my brother Nat home.
He stared right past us as the train pulled in,
from the same window where he last said goodbye,
where he had waved his cap as long as we could
see it, 'til the train curved into the winter fog
bulging like a coachwhip that swallowed a chick.

Hahira welcomed Nat home with a banner and
bluegrass band playing "Sweet Sunny South." He
eased off the steps shouldering a duffel bag big as me,
tanned so dark, spread wide, like men on our mother's
side, a tall wet oak reaching out so high above me
that I could have swung from a rope.

His chest was all decked out in stripes and silver.
I found his Purple Heart. The brass buttons said U.S.
on them. "U.S. for us!" I shouted and held his wrist
tight with both hands. His other hand sat curled near
his ear, on the duffel he would not pass down to Daddy.
Everybody wanted to shake his hand but he wouldn't let go
of mine and walked so fast we left them all behind.

We welcomed him home with fried fish, scuppernong wine
and pie from scratch, blackberry. I picked them that morning
when they were still wet but warmed up a little in the sun.
That's the juiciest time. They were big as my thumbs.
Papaw set catfish hooks the night before, something he had

always meant to do. He and Nat came home with
two dozen mudcats and government-speckleds.

After supper we sat out on the porch and watched
the dirt daubers sip from the bird bath, up and down like
helicopters. Before dark the ducks and geese tramped home
straight into their pen and Mama wired the door shut top and
bottom. Deep in the woods a shotgun went off. Nat stood up and
reached for his belt. The hounds started barking and howling.
"Look, Nat," whispered Mama, "a lightning bug,
the first one I've seen this summer."

I pretended it was and ran out to catch it.
"It's for you." I pried opened Nat's hand but
it curled back into a fist. He wiped it on his pants.

"I'll get you another one," I said.
"Let Nat finish his tea," said Papaw.

The road turned white as the moon rose. It was orange as rust
by day but something made it glow at night. You could see things
coming from far away. "Remember Nat, that time when you and
Mamaw thought there was two kids walking up the road
and you started towards them but it was pumas?"

"Let Nat finish his tea," said Daddy.
"Yeah, ya'll showed them lions—nothin' but ass and elbows!"

That got a grin out of him.

"Remember when Mamaw rode the gopher turtle?"
"I said let Nat finish his tea."
"Naw, I like memories," said Nat. "That's what they're for."

Jill Hoffman, "Washington Square Park," 2011. Oil on canvas, 30" x 40"

Charmagne Sarco

SAFE ROUND WORLD

Sometimes I think the saddest thing I've ever seen
was when my brother Bobby and T.C. Hazelton
were flinging a yellow butterfly back and forth
like a frisbee on T.C.'s crummy dirt street.
Everytime it tried to get away one of them
chucked it back zig-zagging like
the turkey did when Daddy wrung its neck.

I stayed behind a pine tree crawling with
those big black ants and wanted to save
that butterfly more than anything but didn't
let them see me. Partly I think because I loved
Bobby. I never knew him to harm a thing. He cried
after accidently shooting a blue jay with his BB and
when his grasshopper died from the mosquito spray.

But the butterfly didn't die right away.
It took a while to where it couldn't fly so far
or high, like it was getting heavy. The boys
stepped closer and closer together until it just
fell on the ground and started to crawl and
I understood it was never going to make it and
the boys were laughing which made it all
the worse. I ran away. I didn't want to wait
around to see if they stomped on it.
That would of just made me vomit.

I still wonder how they'd of looked if I'd just
run up and kicked T.C. in the nuts, cussed Bobby

you shit ass fuck. I would of cupped that butterfly
in both hands making a safe round world for us,
run through the field into the backwoods, hid
behind the oak tree I always did when I ran away.
Waited until it got its strength back, dripped a little
dew on its stuck-out tongue, straightened its broken
legs with a soft dandelion, stroked its antennas until
they curved up again. Looked into its yellow
cat eyes, smiled and said you are with me now.

It would of pumped its wings up and down
like they do in the sun on honeysuckle.
There was a black eye spot on each one.
If they had enough powder and weren't too tattered
maybe it would of flown off if I'd stood up
and held my hand high as I could.
I'd of even climbed the tree on my elbows and
knees to get to where the wind was, to help it along
until it was on its own gliding down to
the blooming mimosas and hedge of wild roses.

But I just sat up there alone. The yellow moon
crept up behind me. I never told anybody, not even
Bobby. I should of at least gone back for it and
dug a grave, put it in a match box coffin like we did
the grasshopper. I could have made a clover and violet
bouquet, done it right here under this oak tree.
Nothing went right on that day.
Just the same I still loved Bobby.

Jeff McRae

THE LESSON

My grandfather didn't know, did he, my back—
its vulnerable small, where the trunk twisted—
he didn't know my small was like an old man's.
He came to deliver nine birthday spanks.
But I knew the signals muscle and nerve sent,
learned them on the wrestling mat, mismatched
at the meet with an older kid from another school
whose ribs rippled beneath the singlet, whose chin
was razor burn red. There was no calling it off
though I was terrified, in tears, too scared
to beg. We squared up. The whistle blew
and I ran at him. He brushed me aside.
I ran again. This time he gathered me
in his arms, threw me to the mat, fell on me,
locked me in a cradle while my coach shouted
from somewhere and I twisted to execute
an escape. But I was pinned, dominated,
back sprained. So when my grandfather
held me down I panicked, screamed *get off!*
slapped his arms away. And he, not knowing
anything, stood, said something wounded
as an adult will do when a child places his mistake
before him, and walked from the house to the barn
not speaking to me for five days: me who wanted
to know everything like the old man seemed
to know everything; who died to hear the story
about his handstand on the roof of the barn;
or the one where he fell under the truck

and lived to tell it; or the one where he fought
four sailors who whistled at his first wife.
For five days I went to school, rode the bus,
fearing the jolt of every hole. Five days
we did chores in silence, side by side:
one washed and the other dried milk machines.
I watched him pull the levers of the silo motor,
start the serpentine belt that snaked silage
over the feeders, dumping the humid, sweet hay.
I listened to the elevator grind in the silo,
watched the cows dart at the trough,
slamming their skulls together.
Then I hobbled past the herd to where he stood
through the shit and piss that lay everywhere
and begged his forgiveness.

Jeff McRae

BACK WAY

The day after Thanksgiving crows peck a gnarled rabbit
on the old town road up Bates Hill. My father and I,
returning from the store, take this sudden detour
into the trees and hills thick with images: rutted farms,
smoking chimneys, cattle mired in mud. To us
it's a peek behind our lives where nothing seems
as good as it used to be: that barn needs
a new roof; this one is too small for that breed:
we see the folly in the plans of people who do not
share what experience convinced us to be true.
We tell it all in tones of knowing better, staring
at a misery of struggle, dirt, and poverty winding
through the hollow. It is a quarter century since
my father sold up and moved us off the farm.
The falling apart is long over and we are experts
over what we no longer own: the mountainside
and river, a road named for us, for me, for him,
his parents who cut the timber, pulled the stones
from the field; who drained the swales, dug
the run-off; who raised the barns and purchased
the herd; who fed the herd and raised children,
and cleaned trout in the springhouse; who tried
chickens, pigs, a horse, kept a bull; who rotated
cattle from "the hidden piece" to "the night pasture".
We kept two long-handled shovels, hoes, a pitchfork
propped in a garage corner. Now a stick of stove wood
remind us of Jerseys. And then we're home. Soon
we're seated at the table playing cards and drinking

coffee when a car pulls into the yard. Someone's here,
I say. *Who is it?* he asks. I don't know—you find out,
it's your house. *Oh, you know who that is?*
It's the fucking Mormons or some Christly group,
he says, and walks outside. When he returns I ask,
What did they want? *I don't know. They had
their Bibles on their laps and said we need to end
suffering in the world. They told me I was suffering.*
Is that right, I say. What did you say? He settles
into his chair and nods toward the window.
You can see them pulling out the driveway can't you?

Kyoko Uchida

VAN GOGH'S SUNS

Night falls with a slow cry
more animal than woman,
not fearful or despairing, not
yet, but alarmed, alarming.

I lean out into the abandoned
intersection below. Nothing
moves. It is rush hour.
Spindly maples are putting on

their pale pollen glow. Streetlamps
flicker on acid-yellow and inside
cages of tightly woven branches
burn spinning like Van Gogh's suns.

Kyoko Uchida

FORGIVE ME IF I THINK OF MARRIAGE

As a four-legged thing, a sixty-pound mongrel taken in
with fierce resignation. This is going to be messy, I'd said,
having watched a twice-divorced ex-boyfriend paper-train a puppy.
But ours would be different, so the argument always goes:
nearly grown already, spayed, unexpectedly house-trained.
In any case it was too late, half-wild as we were

for her mismatched hurricane eyes.
I was the one who went to the obedience classes
you signed us up for, kept to all the rules you broke
for love. She was the one who kept me company nights
until you came home, then followed you upstairs to bed
while I stayed up reading.

I was the one who took her weekly to the vet,
held her head against my shoulder and the needle
in place, which you could not bear to see.
The prognosis was good until it wasn't.
I stood on the scale with her, then without, figured
the difference, our chances, all the numbers failing.

Those last October weeks when you were away
I slept an hour at a time at the edge of the bed, awake
before she touched my hand. When there was nothing
to be done I asked the vet to wait until you'd seen her.
He was the one who said, *We do not wait to end suffering.*
Yet how she lit up like a sparkler at the sight of you,

pulled herself up for one more walk; you'd think
I'd lied to hurry you back. Then again, she was
more yours than mine. As she should be:
You were the one she favored,
the one she followed
out of the room.

Paul Wuensche, "Self-portrait in a Convex Mirror," 2014. Oil on canvas, 28" x 26"

Mark Kraushaar
7 NORTH, INTERNAL MEDICINE

We'd left her best friend—
bad luck in his lungs—when, suddenly,
a chatty, fat lady in slippers and robe crashed
her double-wide wheelchair into a priest who half
crumpled, half keeled back banging
his head on the gleaming steel
cart by the stairs.
A lady from housekeeping called
for a nurse and an aide came over but the priest
just lay in his inky heap, a little pee
slowly pooling at his hips.

Of course, Mary was quiet,
she was always quiet, but she was quiet.
In a minute though crossing the lobby
she paused and she said, I guess we go along.
She said, And here's this whole unlikely bright life
before us and something happens and something
happens after that so we make a bridge
between them and that's where we are,
we're on this bridge
and underneath us the long days gurgle and surge
and turn into years and we want to get a grip, that's true,
except there's nothing to grasp: oh, love,
and luck, books, places and pets, yes, but which are never
enough, or not really, and every evening on the tv
comes the news and we lean forward to listen, or

we keep reading or talking or typing because
we think we need something to think,
or someone to thank or someone to blame.
But you know how it is, there's clouds and trees
and traffic and laughter then one day you're winding
your watch, or packing a lunch and comes a cough
or a crack and that's that.

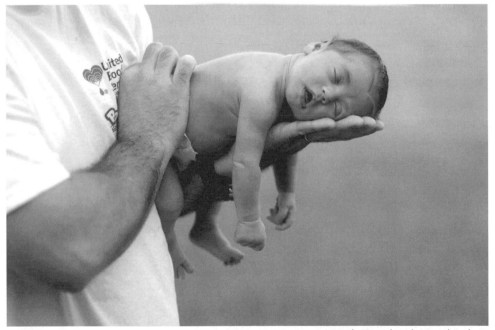

Laura Hetzel, "David and Avigail," photo

Rafaella Del Bourgo
A GIFT

Sometimes you remember to love how the moon organizes the oceans. Sometimes you forget to love. Sometimes you are so caught up being the wheel, whipped around by life, you forget to be the still axis. Sometimes you remember her life – how kaleidoscopic it was, how quietly imperfect. Sometimes you remember her long illness, her death. You wear her watch and feel her pulse beating in your wrist.

Your life, too, has been composed of tessellated bits: meals, trips, jobs, books, men whom you have followed like a gypsy, or one of those wind-up toys which hits a wall and careens off in another direction. Once, lying on the couch, your head on her lap as she brushed your hair, you heard her tell a friend, *Sometimes I think this is not my daughter; she is so dark and beautiful, so bright and so brash, the gypsies must have left her on our doorstep.*

You scuff along the beach for hours. Sometimes you hear a voice, a laugh. You look to your right and are surprised not to find her there. The wind blows hair into your eyes which tear up. You see waves of wild foam after a storm, fragments of smoke-colored clouds against the sky which has been rinsed to a sharp and bewildering blue. Overhead, a hungry osprey on the wing. Glinting in her talons, a wriggling fish. She will tear it to pieces for her nestlings.

You walk around a small harbor, sand gritty between your toes, and halyards ring against sailboat masts. In passing, a woman, a stranger, hands you an unbroken shell. It is conical, silver and rose — the colors of dawn.

Garth Pavell

LOITERING NEAR CHURCH

I was hoping to pick up a girl at one of those
Watered down yet hard to swallow AA meetings

In back I spotted a brunette that seemed to have
Plenty still in her to properly resist arrest

Through the most wickedly beautiful
Eye contact in the seeing world

She told me to fuck myself
Like there was no tomorrow

During the coffee break she picked
At my prepackaged conversation

Jimmied the lock on a few choice words
Until she found something palpable

We slipped out and got a six-pack
It felt wrong giving her tall boys

Down by the old train tracks
Covered in weeds stinking of gin

But it was April and the night
Was quiet and cool, we sat on

The tracks not far from the unborn

Garth Pavell

Mosquitoes and watched her gulp

My story of bad luck blues when all
Of a sudden the mouths of our minds..

Spoke the essence she said was
God yawning ajar the daybreak

We crushed our cans and threw
The forgotten languages of man

Into the bushes that seemed to be
In a trance, waiting too for a long shot

Conor Bracken
BURNING

The star above my front yard is indifferent
to the plight of pale skin too sensitive for sunscreen,

but always on time, a beautifully punctual yellowness.
I was too early at the office campus so I found the ground

and read a book about a man on drugs
that made me feel like I was on drugs

and by this I knew it was good.
By this sign you will know me

she'd said, by the rumpus in the tower
but I didn't have my dictionary,

I'd left my glasses in the restroom
when we were herded to the exits

so the building could shimmy on
its special new coat of flames.

Men in backpacks gathered lawn waste
into shifty piles. Simple things repulsed me,

like body glitter and missed belt loops.
The bus fare had been cheap but not free

though someone tells me that at this place
they used to study space flight.

Now it's all shale analysis and natural gas deposits –
from the ether to the pith, she may say,

the ethereal to the buried. She was beautiful
even before I knew her name

but then I had it and it was a locket I could open
anytime I wanted to go blind with wanting.

Birds swooped and dove, chasing one another through the air
between the fluffed green lollipops. They chirped to each other

things I didn't understand. I burned
their ancestors to get here.

Elisabeth Murawski

IN CHANGING LIGHT

Beside the bed
a torpedo of oxygen.
Children came and went
with big eyes.
My mother didn't cry.
Like Chouchou,
Debussy's daughter,
she kept her tears inside.
We lived so far away
from the farm,
I barely knew her,
my mother's mother.
She adored Lena Horne
in Stormy Weather,
and didn't much like
my father. Before
I was born, Daddy
had a dog named King
who protected him
with his teeth.

Danny Burdett

CORPS DE BALLET – U.S. 101

The birch trees stand
like ballerinas in
close groups. Stark
and slender, white-ensconced,
unholdable. Leaning slightly,
expectantly. Waiting

for their prompt in the
fade of March's unknowable
overture. A tickle in the
root; vibration waving
through the foot. The baton

drops, the heart pumps.
The leaf knows.

Susan Biegler

DESCENDING

At that moment, having
said goodnight, turning down her

lamplit hallway, I heard
feather-steps behind me, swish

of skirt, no slip. A single moth
fluttered about the mahogany landing

settling on a gilt edge. As she
spoke, her upper lip moistened

and my eyes fixed onto the wallpaper
pattern of robed goddesses plucking zithers.

I realize now she wanted to be kissed.
She wanted me to kiss her.

Valentina Gnup

HOTEL AUBADE

The sheets have begun to smell of sex—
      the musky breath of perfume and permission.

In every room we stay I imagine its previous tenants
      —a woman slipping off her red leather pumps,

a man dropping his watch and coins on the nightstand.
      Like any lovers they fill and empty each other;

they sleep on separate sides of the mattress,
      holding the wounds of memory close as a quilt.

At daybreak the man rises first. He kisses the woman's
      shoulder and leaves the room. He returns with apricots

and a baguette he steals a bite from on his way upstairs.
      She stands in the bathroom and studies her reflection

in the narrow mirror—like any woman, she cannot decide
      if she is monstrous or beautiful.

Jim Nawrocki

SOLEMNITY

for my brother

I was glad the old song ended
and that we trailed out into silence.

It was August. Traffic whirred
obscenely beyond us

and the coffin slid so neatly
into its rack, the black door

shut so snugly, that I thought:
The world has become too practiced.

I wanted to leave that row of cars,
walk away alone across the asphalt,

over what was once our playground,
out to where it gave way to grass and

the route I used to take home, a path I'd mapped
behind those cheap apartments, the fence

with the hole in its mesh. Yes,
this is my prayer for now, and for always,

because the litanies and blessings have ended,
and I've chosen as holy, instead, that pause

after the leaves have whispered in their heights
and fallen silent, and I'm walking now

alongside the slumbering creek and winding road
to the hill that ascends to our street,

the row of houses that ends with ours, where out back
the weathered fence still rattles between the yards.

Once, in another life, we had a world here,
and watched the sky like an evolving mystery,

and even the small things were vast.
You were splayed on the grass,

no one, not them, not me, within sight,
only you alone and brilliant

arms spread under your firmament,
unmoored and adrift in your river,

mouthing those mute words
that are only yours.

Rob Sulewski

FRIEND

(after Walahfrid Strabo)

Astonished nights the sky wears no necklace,
only a shining moon so magnificent,
it could be pouring daylight distilled and warm, that moon.

Hear it calling us, its arms soon around us:
friends separated yet fondly mortised.

Grant me at least your pledge
in the liquor of that moonlight.

Hear me whisper my little honest verses to
you—loyal one, iron one—
strong enough for the joys that clutter eternity.

Naomi Rose Howell

LITTLE WOMAN

When grandpa would go out to the store he'd say See You Later, Mac, which is what you called each other and you would embrace like he was leaving for war, which he had done in '42 and I stayed with you five weeks that summer, every night you would squeeze me so I couldn't breathe, you would say I love you to pieces My Little Lamb Chop, and I looked into your watery eyes and knew that you did because when I was in the bath you would always walk by the bathroom and tell me to sing so you could be sure I hadn't drowned. You didn't tell me you were sick, I think you thought I knew but your son never tells us those things and when I saw you for the first time that summer I must have turned white because you said in the cheeriest voice you could muster it's still me, dear, it's the same old me! But the hole in your neck oozed, I saw it, and grandpa helped you clean it and you didn't tell me you were going to die but you did, so I never got a chance to tell you how much I, too, adore Audrey Hepburn and how you were just like all ninety pounds of her. Doe-eyed dancer full of love, swan neck, tiny waist, and the longest feet you'll ever see on a woman.

Francis Klein

HERSCHEL SCHACTER

I was never free of the camps.
The Little Lager left its stain
on the ceiling, spreading
water and blood.

I stared down from my bunk
on the stacked wooden plans.
His peace was not for me,
God, the ritual slaughterer.

I knew the uniforms
of the ghosts.

A dry sea parted
the living from the dead.
A shochet
cleared the coasts.

I am alive
when you hear me,
Mother and Father, fearful
shadows in the loess.

John McKernan

I NEVER MET A COAL MINER

I didn't like   They speak Good
English   I listen hard & am surprised

"The gliders over Holland landed in ditches."
"There're not at all many Republicans
In the Union: Just a few & they don't talk."

"The Coal Camp was picture pretty.
I was there to hear the fresh cut logs
Hammered into houses   I still remember
The smells of the different paints: White

Gray   Blue   Green."   "I always had good bosses.
No one tried to dig me to an early grave.
Free Medical.   A dollar a ton.   I'd do ten tons
Eat a bit   Drink some wine   Take a nap   Then
Back to work. $20 was a fortune.

I took up Barbering cause the work was steady."

John McKernan

TWO A.M. FIRST DAY OF A NEW YEAR

The clock makes
No sound

Outside
All the trees
Wear white snow & white moonlight

Twenty three years ago
After chugging a pint of cherry vodka
I woke up on a park bench
Wearing a blanket of ice on my parka

I shivered for five hours walking home
Thinking of the backhoe
That would dig my grave
In the frozen ground
Not a scrap of that morning was a poem

Laura Weeks

TSVETAEVA'S CHAMBER POT

Maybe, the best victory
Over time and gravity
Is just to slip by, and leave no trace,
To slip by, and leave no shadow
On the wall...
To disintegrate, and leave no earthly dust
     Marina Tsvetaeva

To let: one room. Three flights up. No bath.
A squalid quarter of Clamart.
And there, dead center of the room,
round and redolent, and brimful,
a chamber pot.

An oversight? Maybe you hoped
as you hunkered down at night
after a meal of horses' testicles,
given the general stench of Parisian slums,
it would go overlooked?

Strange. You who preached
the clean getaway – "slip by and leave no trace" –
left this most life-affirming dung.
You, who ordered verbs around like serving girls –
balked by the verb "to be."

A tribute to things physical? Or a rebuke

from the body you so lightly wore –
a paper doll's dress suspended by thin tabs –
and just as lightly shed.

Jill Hoffman, "Shames and Idle Hours," 2014. Oil on canvas, 16"x 28"

Ed McManis

DROWSY

The dreams are
            prophetic
usually in threes.

There is a symmetry
            on the mystic side
of the curtain.

God likes lines.

Your sleeping daughter
            safe in the
radiating nimbus of her

prayer, the mystery of
            virginity
creeping through her freshman class.

The errant arc
            of your only son,
his paucity of

grace, bad aim,
            indelibly stained
nicotine fingers pinching,

miming the spark-
            plug gap,
that left hand of God.

Once, drunk with
        your wife
she giggled and said:

"Heaven's probably a giant
        family re-union
with no booze."

And you offered something
        about epistles
and apostles the infinity

of forgiveness
        bad
potato salad.

The dreams are
        emphatic
how you unzip your

chest each night
        rummage
 for your soul

how your trembling fingers
        reach
into the wound

        to touch

Grace Beekman

PIANO

For thirty minutes everyday
for eighteen years my hands
grew with the keys
and my teacher
the concert pianist
who fled Korea
and an abusive husband
to America with her two
little girls my sister's age
taught me in her broken
but beautiful English:
there are no wrong notes
or right notes — just each
right during one measure
and wrong during another.

J.R. Solonche

THE HORSES

Eight million died in World War I.

They would have needed 8,000,000 men
for one man to apologize to one horse.

When the men did not do so to one another,
where would they have found men to apologize to the horses?

It would have taken 8,000,000 Picassos
to do justice to the death agony of 8,000,000 horses.

Of the 8,000,000 horses, how many had names?
The Germans in particular targeted the horses.

When a British soldier's was killed or died,
he was required to cut off a hoof from his horse

to prove to his commanding officer that they
had not simply been separated, he and his horse.

Too tired to lift their heads high enough to breathe,
they drowned in the deep mud, thousands of the horses.

Because they were used to draw the artillery,
the most losses were suffered by the Clydesdale horses.

For some countries, the largest commodity
shipped to the front was fodder for the horses.

J.R. Solonche

Because saw dust was mixed with their food,
they starved to death, thousands of the horses.

Gasmasks were issued for the horses,
but they destroyed them, mistaking them for feed bags.

The better-bred horses suffered from shell shock
more than the less well-bred horses.

These learned to lie down at the sound of the guns.
They were sold to the French butchers, the surviving horses.

Jane Woodman

ADIRONDACKS

My mother picked me up from kindergarten,
Day One, wearing a crew neck sweatshirt
with four pastel Adirondack chairs lined up

on the front - arms outstretched, one knee
in the gravel, easy for me to leap in from the blur
of lunch lines and that giant custodian.

She always had such faith in September –
little sprouts tottering off to dinosaur habitats,
yellow brick roads, the moons of Saturn.

If only all school buses were magic ones,
every skinned knee healing in time
to pan for fake gold in the bushes.

If all lima beans could know the dirt
around them would be patted into place
by not one, but two gentle sets of hands.

Jade Sylvan

BLOOM

If I had to carve my most romantic 24 hours it would be in the bloom of last May in Portland, the Rose City, when a woman I'd just met said yes, played hooky, borrowed a car and drove to meet me. She brought me a flower picked deep in the forest and her name meant flower, too, come to think of it, but I'm trying not to fall in love with people for their names anymore. After spicy cocktails we lay on a queensized floor mattress in the hall outside the room her exhusband shared with his boyfriend. She asked if I thought there was such a thing as a soul and instead of answering I asked if I could kiss her. The next morning her ex cooked us breakfast. Duck eggs from his own backyard ducks. That day we held hands on every Western street in the city. Found food trucks that served brown rice. She looked like Regina Spektor but I'm trying not to fall in love with people who remind me of fictional characters, dead people, or celebrities. Everyone I meet reminds me of fictional characters, dead people, or celebrities. That day was magic, say the movies. Thick West Coast double-fist coffees and a frivolously purchased floppy hat. Hours sitting cross-legged in the religion section of Powell's. I've never had a lover for spring. Before everything started in the dead times. I'm trying not to fall in love with anyone who reminds me of a season. She'd only ever been east of Colorado once, on a roadtrip to New York City. It was too large and too grey, she said. In Eugene she lives deep in the forest, has a barn and a goat named The Goat. I'm trying not to fall in love with people for their houses. She wants to quit everything and sit on her back porch and write tiny private poems about flowers. Flowers make my nose run. Always have. They're still beautiful and necessary. I'm trying not to jump ahead and imagine all buds wilting. Trying to enjoy the skull's gorgeous trudge through the face's smiling flesh. We know how it ends. I'm trying not to not let my story of us outpace our breathing. I'm trying to hear more than my own voice. In May we each take pictures of flowers, pink magnolia, yellow tulip, purple triteleia. Scatterfloat them across 3000 miles to each other's palms. I'm trying not to conjure glamour alongside these clumsy, unfashionable bodies. I'm trying not to tell any story but yes.

Jack Herz, "Nude on Pink," 2012. Oil on canvas, 30" x 40"

Andy Roberts

SAILING WITH THE SPIDER

Boredom, disgust with news on the radio
drive me into the basement where my dead father's
suits hang on a metal conduit between two joists.
I select a gray pinstripe, blow off the dust,
slip on the jacket three sizes too big.
From the left inside pocket a bulge, familiar smell.
I pull out a meerschaum pipe, packet of
Black Velvet tobacco. The chewed mouthpiece
hasn't felt lips in over forty years
till I clamp it in my teeth, take a dry hit,
fail to gag. I pack a bowl, strike a match,
blow out a white stream of Black Velvet
to the spider in the joists. I take another hit,
accidentally inhale sickly sweet burnt tobacco,
sailing somewhere out of my head
with the spider, the dust,
cuffs sliding over my fingers.

Andy Roberts

THE EASY SEASON

What can be done in the easy season? –
breaking my fast with black coffee and fried eggs,
the newspaper's lies,
ghosts in the radio mumbling and sighing,
the hurricane spinning its long arms of rain.

Soon I will wade through tall weeds to the pond
humming with horseflies, feet in the mud,
searching the cattails for spiders,
the whites of my eyes like bowls of soup
as I float on my back, lids closed against bright sun.

In summer I sweat for my weekly paycheck,
spitting midges from my mouth,
clawing cobwebs from my face,
hacking the purple thistle, milkweed, queen anne's lace,
then cutting a hollow reed to breathe through.

And each night I return to the house for a schooner of beer
and a nap in my easy chair with a breeze through the window,
my green house plants crawling toward light,
the dust in the corners of the hardwood floors,
the dark paneled walls filled with pictures of all those I love.

Mary Ann Mayer

RINGO, WHAT AM I LIVING FOR?

That year of stray jobs,
the year I felt irrelevant,

I got interested in canine dermatology—
one night in Providence, at the Met Cafe
leaning on a lolly column
akimbo to the stage, listening

to a country-grunge singer,
sing about the general idea of a goal in life.

Anyway, that's what I read into the lyric of white roses
appliquéd across his dingy satin shirt,
three bottom snaps undone, pouty belly
popping out, the rest of him – Jagger-thin –

all liquored up, humping the mike stand, crooning,
"I'm so miserable I almost want you back".

Flo, the bar dog, ambles back and forth in front of the stage.
One haunch mangy, the other hairless from lying in swill;
I lean a little straighter,
more awake to life's possibilities.

Canine dermatology!
I call her over for a scratch but she's gone off with the bouncer.

I light up in bars. Get ideas. Like Ringo.
Who knew he'd composed more songs than Lennon-McCartney?
Problem was, he said, he couldn't read his own handwriting in the morn-
ing.
Me, I'd kill for that collection.

That's what canine dermatology must be like.
A shot at resurrection. The chance to dig
Flo's dew-claw, hooked and ingrown, out of her leg
see tears of gratitude fill her brown bedroom eyes

Laura Hetzel, "Deer skull at my father's camp," 2013. Photo

Michael Graves
SPREAD

When I gazed at the photos
Of the naked young woman
Who sold herself to Spitzer
And saw her calculating eyes,
Though I had thought to titillate myself,
I knew why I did not rise.

"Yalta Conference at the Jewish Cemetery,"
30x40 inches, mixed media

Meg Eden

WHAT I'VE LEARNED FROM WATCHING ZEE TV

In high school, Miti brings saris in the morning
and we change in the bathroom stalls
while the first bell goes off. We skip
through the halls, arms linked, singing
the lyrics to Bollywood songs
that the white girls don't know.

Because I don't think of myself as one
of the white girls—I think of myself
as dark like the henna Miti presses
onto my hand. I think of my eyes
heavy and strange in a world
of girls in bootie shorts.

Miti works late shifts at Subway
even though she's a religious vegetarian,
and dates a boy six years older than her.
Yesterday, a blonde in art class taught her "fuck"
and she's been saying it whenever she gets the chance.
When she gets perfume, she sprays it fifteen times
around her body until I can find her by smell.

When I get home from class, I watch
Aishwarya Rai movies and wonder
what you have to do to get that beautiful.

Meg Eden

I dance with my fingers close to my head.
I dance like my life is a Bollywood film,
and this is the scene where the heroine
sings about loneliness.

David Potter, "Osaka," photo

G. B. Ryan

NORTHWEST FOREST

I call them hemlocks and redwoods,
trees that darken the afternoon
and make me remember the story of the man who left his car

and walked some yards into the woods
to take a leak and could not find
his way out again, the scattered and chewed bones presumed to be his,

in the twilight of these big trees
in which I feel like a swimmer
suddenly aware of marine possibilities underneath

my kicking legs and flashing skin,
no map, compass, food or water,
no things creeping toward me on furred belly except my own thoughts

Judith Ann Levison

LINEAGE

I would not have told you
If you were going to shudder
Look wounded again at the name given you

A lineage gives you a box of relics
Old eyeglasses, ribbons, a piece of silk
And whirling voices all trying to speak

In drenching rain their tears let you know
Your sorrows were like theirs
In every pattern of a rainbow's floating veins
They said someone had your soft grey eyes

Or even was your twin, sailing in a boat
Her garden hat trailing in the water
Disliking all her eligible men
Wearing a tarnished bracelet
Glinting your names in the sun
Hoping you too found no one

Michael Montlack
PATRON OF THE ARTS

About to graduate with my BA
in Creative Writing, and unsure
what to do with it, my father, picking
pie crumbs from the kitchen table,
said, How bout joining the service?

Service? But I'd recently told him
I was gay. So what? he said.
Don't ask, don't tell—right?
Just think: you could see the world.
On their dime! Plus, it's where
he was trained. As a mechanic.

I was furious, thinking Service?
This man didn't get me at all.
Though it was flattering too—
that he (at 62) could see his gay son
following in such manly footsteps.

After I explained how grad school
was more my speed, he said
he'd help where he could.
But why the poetry? I mean, it won't
pay the bills ... Why not write—
I dunno—a musical?

A musical? But I wasn't a musician!
Or an actor. So what? he said.
You could do it! I bet it'd pay good too.
I saw that 'Guys and Dolls' once.
Great show. Maybe something like that ...

You never took me to a show!
my mother said, clearing the plates.
When in the world did you go
to the theater? While in service—
he finally remembered. (Of course.)
Then gave me a nod. See, kid?
Just another one of the perks.

I tried to outline what I could
only imagine were the intricacies
of creating a musical from scratch.
Bored with the details (or finally
understanding?) he moved on.

How bout a pop-up book then? he said.
My mother perked up. Yes—
you always loved those, Michael!
A pop-up book? Like for kids? But
I wasn't an artist! Or children's writer.
Were they out of their minds?

Yeah, bet there's a good buck

in pop-up books. Could be
a whole career. My mother agreed.
Okay, I said, hoping to lead them
to the inevitable dead end: If I could
figure out how to construct one,
what do you suggest I write about?

I dunno, my father said. Isn't that
the fun part? He paused. Let's say …
let's say … you got a chicken.
A chicken? I said. Yeah, he said.
A chicken—let's say you got a chicken …
There you go! Start from there.

Paul Wuensche, "Dorset sheep", 2014. Oil on canvas, 12"x12"

Michael Montlack

ROME: PERPETUAL WALLS

In a city scattered with the remains
of walls—temples, tombs, stadiums—
my bed-and-breakfast host Mario
drew for me in the air another wall,
the one his mother had insisted on
back in '43 in their Trastevere home.
Yes, just a few blocks away! His father
didn't question her, just split one
of their rooms in a way the Nazis
wouldn't detect: Our apartment
strange already. Medieval, ya know?

A sealed box but for a hole to feed
and water them, that family of eight
who had lived downstairs, not believing,
like the other Italian Jews, the worst
until 1,100 were sent to camps that day.
Mario's mother came home to find
her neighbor yellow in the face,
he said. She told her— you no worry!
Then sent Mario's father to work.

But didn't they fear being caught?
I asked. Endangering your own family?

He looked across the kitchen at me
while setting the espresso machine.
No. The people then, they do things

for love. Not just to get something.
My father— he loved my mother. And
my mother—she loved her friend …
The Nazis arrived and didn't buy
the family had gone. So they searched
but found nothing. Just walls.
In those irregularly shaped rooms.

The family lived. And after the war
Mario's mother refused to be featured
in the papers. But when she died
decades later, he said, smiling Our church
was filled with Jews. Jews! So many Jews.

Emily Hipchen
DOG YEARS

The couch smells of dog, this dog
on his side on the floor on our last night together,
but we don't know that yet.
I drift off, one hand on his shoulder, the other
a fist tucked under my head.
I dream. In the dark, one streetlight
like a star picks out the sash, the edge of a table.
I wake up to the wind rushing by,
to the hollow sound of this dog's heart
beating the floor like a tom-tom,
emptying itself of blood, filling, emptying.
His heart is thumping like his tail on the wood floor,
knocking *hello hello you're home at last don't go.*

Paul Wuensche, "Bridge by the fire," 2014. iPhone drawing

Willa Schneberg

UGLY

It is a personal matter for the first and second wife to resolve.

Khieu Thavika - Cambodian government spokesman

I was beautiful too
and gave him sons.
I would sit in his lap
as he fastened gold
bracelets to my wrists.
He took me to Singapore.
There used to be caresses
before he entered me.
My husband is a powerful man,
high up in the government.
Powerful men don't grow old,
like their wives.

He won't replace me
with a bar girl
who sold cigarettes and
bottles of petrol on the roadside.
I will pour a vial of acid
over her head, and then a second
vial, and a third...
He will no longer want her.
She will burn and scream.
I won't stop
until she's
ugly.

Saul Zachary

WALK-UP

In my crowded
empty apartment,
a party's going on.

Stunners in flapper dresses
shimmy to Dixieland,

poems are being written
in invisible ink
and argued over,

my family shouts
terrible truths
about each other
from picture frames,

Nijinsky, costumed
in rose petals, leaps
from my bedroom
through the living room
and out a window

landing softly in the
Manhattan sky between
Orion and the Big Dipper,

while in my place

there's always enough time
for Romeo to find
his destined Juliet,

for my family to make peace
and poems to explode,

even for Nijinsky to leap
back from heaven
if he wants to.

Laura Hetzel, "Sisters", 2014. Photo

Lyn Lifshin

ON THE NEW ROAD

red sumac presses
against the windshield,
tires moan

your wife dreams
you are guilty,

I button and unbutton
what I feel

Jon Schmitt

OVER BREAKFAST

At first we talked of
love as if it were a
mock negotiation,
you saying that given
the right
incentive, you could be made to
see things almost my way.

I didn't feel like I was doing
myself justice, and I made
excuses—
my eyes stung, my throat was sore,
the coffee was cold and tasted like graphite.

But I muddled through, making feints at
certitude, even daring to venture that life
together still meant death all alone.

I really thought at one point I had the upper
hand, until you looked, smiling, out the win-
dow and mentioned that the sky and the
clouds made you think of a blue marble city
being bombed straight to hell.

Elizabeth L. Hodges
SECRET

She can't write it down because it was years
ago and anything she says now would
betray the simplicity of that moment.
Even in her dreams, when she approaches
what seems to be the answer, a blinding
white light falls like a curtain on her
premonitions. To think it would still
bother her after all these years. It
is like imagining that we dream of
falling because we once slept in trees. It
is like saying genius is only born of a
deviate mind. So she sits—
staring at the even blue lines before
she can bring herself to write characters
on the page. Never (it is so impossible)
would she want to see anything of herself there,
acting on the stage.

Simon Perchik

S59

This grave gives thanks and it's sad —her name
hollowed out from the bone in your body
not connected to any other

though help will never come —your throat
gave up everything just to dig itself in
and yet this dirt still changes hands

empties the Earth into a few small stones
already a necklace for this headstone
coming by to make her look her best

as if you were going somewhere together
dressed warm with flowers and kisses
where your arm used to be.

Simon Perchik

S116

Rubbed smooth though grave to grave
what this rock carries inside helps lift it
to see through –the dress, black

then silence then the shoulders
she was buried in, growing wild
the way every mountain bit by bit

waves goodbye as if its belly
is always empty, needs to be warmed
pulled closer, sleeves and all.

Laura Hetzel
MARKING

our mother marked the grave with plaster angels, concrete hearts,
plastic plants, lights at Christmas, everything but a headstone.

I skipped church when I could and hid in the cemetery. it was the only place
I couldn't be found, lying belly down on top of her, matching lengths.

people always ask how a twin can be told from the other twin,
how the mother can know.

my mother writes letters to my dead sister in a journal kept under her bed
you were like me. I see Laura and she is unfeeling

we were one body but how many souls?
no name on the grave after twelve years.

no way to know which one of us they buried

Carl Mayfield

YOUNG MAN IN JAIL

he was 15 going on 42
saying his mother was like
the ocean because she
didn't know how to write

one evening we set aside
the letter to his lawyer
so he could write:
"dear pacific ocean, I know
you are really my mother—"

2 weeks later he yelled
across the room:
"mister, you won't believe it
but I got a letter from the ocean—"
& his face reflected
a light often seen
at the edge of moving water

Mary du Passage
5:25 AM/26 OCTOBER

record everything in NOTES FOR A LOVE POEM standing
never written standing up before
a proper position for thinking straight

Today is Tuesday, no responsibilities beyond to myself
& Lulu. Angele is working at home, Emerson home sick
tho nothing serious.

Tomorrow is Wednesday, thus return to their house
by 4:00 PM when the Christ Episcopal school bus
drops them off by the driveway. First year
I don't pick them up in my black Honda civic
closer now to free as a bird.

Crows are found on every continent save Antarctica.
Crows are the most intelligent of all the birds.
Crows communicate, warn each other of danger.
Crows make eye contact. They watch us, pick a face out
            of a crowd. Watching, learning & remembering.
Crows are opportunistic, as humans, like feeding on garbage
                thus we don't like them. They eat fruit,
                vegetables & meats.
Crows need to be close to each other, especially
                the young with their parents.
Crows mate for life, live as long as 20 years.

A family takes care of its members' needs.

Young crows go off to play, always to return to family safety.
End of adolescence comes at 5 months, close to time
            to choose a mate of their own.

Crow l krō l noun— a large perching bird with mostly glossy
black plumage, a heavy bill & a raucous voice
Genus Corvus, family Corvidae, several species
American crow (brachyrhynchos)
Crow family includes: crows, ravens, rooks, jackdaws, jays,
magpies, treepies, choughs and nutcrackers
Crows are considered the most intelligent of the birds,
and among the most intelligent of all animals

Crow, verb— loud characteristic cry expressing joy or triumph
            eat crow – humiliated having to admit one's error
            old crow – old or ugly woman

R. Steve Benson

SHE WORKED PART-TIME TO HELP OUT

From September to June
her confused children
rode a bright yellow school bus
past this gray pagan place
where tall rogue field corn
still volunteers from cracks
between sunken slabs
of oil-soaked cement.

The nearest town
is a forty mile commute.
You'd think some smart investor,
who didn't believe in
wronged spirits, would
forget about the bad luck
that lingers here
like a rotten odor,
and build a shiny new truck-stop
with T-shirts, bathrooms,
groceries and cheap souvenirs.

For years I stopped here
for gas, pop and candy
when I drove my young son
back to his remarried mother.
The friendly farmwife,
so casually murdered here

R. Steve Benson

during a robbery, enjoyed
joking and laughing with us
about all the junk food
we bought — fluffing
my son's fine blond hair.

But now, when I look around
this desolate country corner,
she is nowhere. All that remains
are weeds and broken glass
and a rusty metal tank
that was dug up from underground
because that's the law now.
You can't leave those
gas tanks buried; they might
poison the groundwater

Danielle Lemmon
THE SEWERS OF PARIS

I google the name of a little boy
I babysat in France. His mother
told me over 25 years ago that
he had an unusual and antiquated
French name so maybe I will find
him and sure enough he's on Facebook
and he has a lot of friends with French names,
which surprises me, because I always forget
about the two years I spent living in France.

I never even went to see the Eiffel Tower.
I used to take my visitors to des egouts.
I thought a boat ride through the sewers
was such a funny way to see Paris, or not,
and the smell was not too bad.
The only thing that made any sense
to me back then was reading
a biography of Janis Joplin titled
Buried Alive and writing letters
to my friend in Mexico. It was a relief
not to understand the language
that people were speaking around me.
I just sat in cafes, sipping coffee,
and staring out the window.

Until I got the job taking care
of a little boy who acted like an older man.
Soon it was clear that he was taking care
of me. I never had any idea where

we were and he knew the names of all
the subway stops at age three.
Il est tres intelligent, the old lady
sitting beside us declared loudly.
I used to ask him to translate words.
What is it when there is something
in the air and you cannot see clearly?
"Brume, Danielle, ca c'est brume!"
he answered brusquely as if I was a student
who had not done her homework
and should know the word for fog,
even if I was lost in a fog, especially
if I was as lost as I was.

Once when we were eating fish,
he suddenly blurted out, "Des Arretes!
Attention, Danielle, attention!"
He was warning me not to choke
on bones. Toi, aussi, I answered
weakly. I used to tell him stories
to pass the time and prepare him
for all the lies he would encounter
as an adult. I was recovering from some
of those lies as I hid out in Paris. Once,
when we were walking down the Champs Elysees
after swimming in a public pool, he asked me
to carry him. No, my arms are broken, I replied
and showed him the break at my elbows.
"Danielle, tu fait des histoires encore, " he responded
in a weary voice. At least he didn't call me
a liar, only a fabricator of tales.

I heard his mother screaming as I lay
on the bed in my attic room. She had just
discovered that her husband was having an affair
with her best friend. I listened tensely until
his favorite grandfather burst through the front door
calling out his name. "Arnaud! Arnaud!"
"Papi!" he shrieked in agony and relief.
I had to pick him up at nursery school
the next day and he was sitting all alone
in a corner with a big frown on his face.
"Je veux voir Papi," he stated firmly
when he saw me. Papi isn't here.
Only Danielle. He thought for a moment
and then he followed me out the door.

I took him home to listen to Janis Joplin.
We turned the music up high and
chased each other around the furniture
laughing and screaming
louder than Janis.

Alison Jarvis (Reprinted)

ELEGY FOR A DRUMMER

Past midnight, a weeknight, I'm still
sitting in a carved out, windowless place
off Eighth Avenue. The heat

outside's a piston
insisting itself into the dead
center of August. Nobody

smokes anymore. So I just drink
and listen to a trio move through
its predictable paces, waiting

for something to happen.
And then it does – the startlingly
beautiful stolen vernacular

of early Coltrane: Everytime
We Say Goodbye. It doesn't matter
how many years, I'm back –

record on the stereo, empty
bed tracked with makeup
and sweatsalt. Trane

playing in sheets of music
as though single notes
don't exist. The perfect grief

of the sax, and you –
twenty below, four in the morning
high again, coatless – you call

from the booth on the corner –
Baby please – and I'm that woman
in the Czech photograph

Billy sent you from Prague,
the one who stands at a lit window
looking down at a street

so silent she hears
the crash of the milk
before it tilts off the sill.

Your car runs at the curb – exhaust
a white shot of longing
or dread. Snow falls

fine, like dope. You need me
to hold you down making love.
Unanchored you become only part

of the darkness. Breath and smoke
from your cigarette cloud the glass
until your bare hand sweeps

the blurred world into a moment
of focus. My face over yours
a lit whisper, Witness me.

Alison Jarvis

Once you told me
There's no going back.
You can't fix things

in music, you jump into time
then it's over.
I've imagined that

stillness, the half-cold

air of spring. The road endlessly
unspooling against

a gray blur of morning. Even now,
tonight, in this bar,
in the mix of bourbon and perfume,

in the collective, cooled-off sweat
of strangers, tensed against the inevitable
Last Call, Last Call …

I smell the pungent crush
of new grass as your car bears
the sycamore to rest

at its heart. Blossoms burst, leaves
explode, the gone world falls
around you. Blue Train still
playing on tape.

Bill Edmonson

ASHES

For the time, I'll set aside
your unspeakable act. Today
in this heat, in the sweep of
our last natural river,
we will as I have often dreamed
be brothers. Come down to the water
with me. At that cold, hard pour
between two boulders
we'll put him in.

Dropping along the shattered granite trail,
my hold on this cardboard box, heavy
as ingot, is absolute. It takes my hand,
pulls me out of balance.

Kneel here in the wet river sand, cool
as a compress. Open the box. Cut open
the plastic sack. On the opposite bank
an innocent family picnics.

Do I have something to say?

This: He was a good father and a good
man. As near as I know,
whatever faith he had,
he kept.

In my dream,
he stood on this same river
I've seen him fish a hundred times,
then silently laid down his rod,
took off his hat and
without looking back—still holding it—
jumped in. I started forward
then woke.

Now we can undertake it.
Now there's no breeze to fluster the ash.

The ceremony eats my strength,
and drinks I've drunk come on.
All's bright, heightened.
Green and blue, the diamond glint
of sunlight scattered across surface
I see my car high up on Howland Road.
It glows, a coal.

Even you can't know the reasons
you sledged our friendship of over forty years,
you can only say you were "attracted."
Brother, old friend, bastard rat,
it just won't wash.

Jill Hoffman
RIVAL MYTHS

I wanted to call Maddy on her birthday. September 25th. In fact, I had planned to call her a month before her birthday to break the ice. We hadn't spoken for a long time. But I forgot. Every year on my birthday she sent me a beautiful gift. The last was an antique silver pin, a mermaid with startled hands who looked as if she were flying. But this year I hadn't heard from her.

I was driving in Connecticut with Jack when I remembered that I hadn't called her. "I think I missed Maddy's birthday," I said. "It's the 25th. " I was upset. It wouldn't be the same to call late.

"It's the 25th today," Jack said. "Call now."

I got out my cell. And my address book. I didn't have her number in the cell. A man answered. I thought maybe it was her son. "William?" I asked.

"No. Tsering," he replied.

He had an accent. I thought she was having a late affair like I was. She had finally found a man, burly perhaps, in a flannel shirt, who stayed in her house and helped her.

"Is Maddy there?" I said.

"Yes. Do you want to talk to her?"

"Happy Birthday, for god's sake," I said when she got on the phone.

She laughed. It was good to hear her voice. She sounded younger, mirthful. The last time we had spoken she had said not to come to California because her friends from the dog run were making a birthday party for her. 'That's so nice,' I said, but I was offended. Before that she had had a fall, in her own backyard, and been hospitalized. I always fell, I told her. She hadn't gone into details. "Who is this?" she said.

"Jill. Your best friend in the world."

She laughed some more. "Yes, it's my birthday," she said. "It's very kind of you to call. Where are you?"

"Connecticut."

"I'm in Connecticut too."

"You are? That's unbelievable. Where in Connecticut?"

"I'm a little confused today. My mind has been on — other things. Tell me about your life."

"Well, I'm painting, and trying to find a dealer, and the harder I try the less I succeed," I said. She understood, I could tell by her sympathetic chuckles. "Where in Connecticut are you?" I asked.

There was a weird silence. "Where am I?" she finally asked the man. 'Santa Rosa,' I heard him say. "I'm in Santa Rosa," she said.

"That's California."

"I meant to say California," she said. "Why don't you come over now?"

"I can't. I'm in Connecticut. I knew you were in Santa Rosa."

"You did? How did you know?"

"That's where you live."

She made a dismissive noise, as if to say, *not really.* "Most of the time I'm in Afghanistan, or someplace."

"How is your dog, Prince Hal?" His other name was Hallelujah, I remembered. She was a dog person, like me.

"He died."

"That's terrible. How? Why?"

"He just died."

"When?"

"Three or four months ago."

That's terrible," I said again.

"Yes, it was terrible," she said gravely. "Where are you now?"

"Connecticut. I'm still with Jack."

"I'm living in the house my mother used to live in, only my sister has taken it over."

I never met her younger sister. "I didn't know that," I said. I imagined a dark legal squabble. "The house your mother gave you?" Her mother had sold it to her for a dollar.

"I suppose she gave it to me. . . . I don't know where my mother is living. I don't know if she's alive or dead," she muttered. I was stunned. Now it was clear. For a moment I had forgotten that her sister had died a few years ago. Maddy had told me that she had gotten close with her sister right before she died. I couldn't remember what her sister died of. Drugs and alcohol, or cancer.

It was as if I was the one with Alzheimer's.

"That's how I feel about my mother sometimes," I said. I had guilty dreams that I hadn't visited her and she was alive. But Maddy was living in a bad dream she couldn't wake up from.

"Your mother died," I said. "She was in her eighties." She had had to take chemo for a second time and Maddy had worried that it was dangerous for someone in her eighties, not like it was for me.

"She did? When?

"Many years ago."

"Really?"

"Yes."

"Where are you now?"

"Connecticut."

Jack gave me a strange look. I was repeating 'Connecticut' a lot. Now I didn't know if her dog had died, or not. Maybe they had taken the dog away and told her that he had died. She had sent me pictures of the dog, a black and white spotted poodle.

"How long have we known each other?" she asked.

It seemed a nostalgic question, as if she were cognizant of the value of long friendship.

"Since 1955. How long?" I asked Jack.

"Fifty-six years," he said.

"Fifty-six years," I said.

"That's a long time," she said. It was a long time. We had met at Bennington on our first day there. and had been best friends ever since.

"How is William?" I asked.

"He's making movie after movie, and travelling the world. He's very successful. He's a valuable intelligent person and I love him very much." This sounded completely normal. It was what she always said. She lived for her son. William had made a documentary on Buddhism, and had also lost a hundred thousand of Maddy's money on the stock market.

"I'll come visit you," I promised.

"Why don't you come now? I'd like to talk to you — and Jack."

"I can't. I'm in a car in Connecticut, driving past all the pretty houses, going to Bed, Bath and Beyond to buy a peppermill. It's pretty in Connecticut," I said.

"Oh, I know," she said.

"Who is the nice man you're with?" I asked.

"You're right. He is a nice man – very smart. But he's not *with* me."

"Oh."

"Where do I know you from?" she said.

Maddy knew Greek. She had come straight from her junior year in high school, without graduating, with a Greek library, and early American furniture and art. I still remembered one cracked oil painting of peanuts on a table that resembled sheep, or sheep in a brown meadow that resembled peanuts. And how I swallowed my disappointment when I lent her my new cashmere sweater dress and got it back stretched and misshapen.

We were sixteen. She was fat like a monk, with a frizzy head of curls. She wore ponchos that she made by cutting a hole in hand-woven blankets for her large head to go through. She glued her very large diaphragm to a canvas and hung it on her wall. It was hers. Her mother had given it to her a long time before.

She had peed on her father's stomach when she was three, and her father had never forgiven her for it. Her parents didn't love her, she told me, because she was fat.

She tried to make love to me once. It was the summer of our freshman year when we spent a month together in Provincetown. We were in a little hut in the sand dunes. It had no floor. It was like a waterbed made out of sand. I flatly refused. "I can't. I couldn't," I said. She might have been disappointed. I know the old beachcomber-artist who had lent us the house for the night, and who was watching through the window, was. He saw my breasts when I changed my clothes. We stumbled upon him as we went out to touch the black ocean, like a giant mermaid wearing barrettes of phosphor in her hair.

That summer, I had stayed at her house for an extended visit. Her parents' house was on the water in Westchester. They had a dachshund, a lawn full of weeping willows, and a cook who served formal meals. Her mother was away for the weekend. Her father was a wiry redheaded man. Clifford Stein.

He sat in a comfortable armchair, drinking. I sat at his feet, fascinated, listening to his banter, the way I sat at my teacher Howard Nemerov's feet in college.

It was late at night. Maddy was tired and went to her room.

"Last night my wife squeezed a pimple in the mirror, right in front of me," Clifford said. He laughed. I was horrified that any woman would do such a thing in front of a man. It impugned all women. I wanted to make the pimple go away, so I let him kiss me.

I forgot that he was married, that he had tattled on his wife, that he was kissing his daughter's friend. I felt I had to earn my keep.

"Time for bed," Maddy's father said a little later and took my hand. I followed him upstairs to his bedroom. There were two twin-sized beds. I glanced past the open bathroom door at the white sink, at his wife's plain robe. He pulled me down next to him on one of the beds. I felt bad about Maddy more than her mother. I was worried that she would hear, that she would know. I was wearing a halter and shorts. He pulled my panties aside under my shorts. The penetration surprised me. I thought we were just flirting.

There was no blood. I didn't think of it as rape. Instead of calling the police, I fell in love.

Clifford drove us to Provincetown the next day. He sang. I sat next to him and memorized his freckles like a mistress. Then he settled Maddy and me in the room with a double bed she had taken for a month, and left.

Maddy knew all the painters in P'town. Franz Kline, Robert Motherwell. We went to a party on our first night there and met Norman Mailer. "Let's have a staring contest," he said to Maddy. Norman Mailer and Maddy stared into each other's eyes. Maddy had pale green eyes, like Zen pools. Norman Mailer and Maddy blinked at exactly the same time. It was a tie. Then Norman Mailer stared into my eyes and I stared back into his. "Have you read my book, *Deer Park*?" he asked. "No," I said. I hadn't even read *The Naked and the Dead*. "Oh, you must read *Deer Park*," he boasted, "it's my best book." I laughed; he won.

That summer I met an artist named Tarr Roads. He was older and missing a side tooth. I lost all interest in Maddy. She complained to her father that I was ignoring her; I was always with the artist. Her father came to P'town but I didn't see him. I never saw him again. By the time school started she and I had made up. I was still seeing the artist.

During parents' weekend, when my parents visited, Maddy was with me in my room. "How would your mother feel if you were dating a non-Jewish man," my mother asked her.

"Fine," she said. "My mother isn't Jewish."

My mother was silent.

"I didn't know your mother wasn't Jewish," I said as soon as we were alone.

"She is Jewish," she said. "It was a lie." I was impressed. She was brilliant, like Gertrude Stein. Howard Nemerov said that Maddy and I were the "two best students" he had ever had.

Long after we graduated, Maddy's mother and father divorced. He married a young woman in England, a minister's daughter. When he was dying, Maddy and her husband dutifully went to England to be with him. It was not a reminder that she wanted his money, her rightful inheritance. It was to show him that she loved him.

From his deathbed, he gave her the finger. Then died.

"My mother won," she told me.

"How? What do you mean?"

"He died first."

I had introduced Maddy to her husband. He was a poor professor, legendary for his golden tongue. He was short, Italian, balding. When we went out for Chinese food, he collapsed on the sidewalk from the MSG. She told me his penis hung down to his knees; she didn't see how she could go wrong. Each dish she prepared for him he called a "poem." He died slowly in the hospital from stomach cancer, a green bottle of bile at his side.

There was a boy I had desperately wanted to marry. When he asked about me, Maddy told him I was "seeing someone else."
"Why did you say that?" I asked her.
"Well, you were," she said.
Maddy's son was born first. She spoiled him. When my daughter was born I had a flash of Maddy in the set of her jaw. It was prophetic: my daughter was a genius. But I stopped seeing Maddy for thirteen years. I didn't want our children to play together; she cared too much about material things. I saw her once on a highway, standing beside her car that had broken down. But she was on the other side of the cement divide and my husband and I didn't turn our car around to help her.
After we made up for the second time, we talked every Saturday. She lived in Vermont. I was always asleep when she called.
One Saturday, she brought up the subject of the time her father drove us to P'town.
"I was very attracted to my father that day," she said.
I was startled. It was bizarre to say such a thing. I almost had to admire her for it; I had never been "attracted" to my father. But then I worried. It was such a specific day. The day he sang in the car. Great teenage fireworks of excitement filling the air. I was afraid she knew everything.
"Was that the only day you were attracted to him?" I asked.
"No," she said. "I always thought that maybe you had slept with my father," she added.

Finally, I admitted that I had.

"You must have told people that you slept with my father."

"No, I didn't tell anyone."

"Well, you certainly must have told Howard Nemerov for one."

"No, I didn't."

"Well, then why did he say to me, 'Your father is a shit'?"

"Probably because of what you told him about your father," I said.

We were like sheep grazing in the brown meadow of the past, or peanuts in their shells on an old table. She had moved to California. It was Saturday; I was asleep. Maddy called.

"I've never told this to anyone before," she said. "But I distinctly remember saying to my father, 'What would you do if I peed on you?'"

"What did he say?" I asked.

"He said, 'I'd spank you.' And then I peed on him, and he spanked me."

"You did tell me a version of this before," I said. "You told me you peed on your father's stomach when you were three, and your father never forgave you for it." I could still hear her saying it, pink and sandy, intellectual, boundaryless.

"I must have been younger than six," she went on, "because it was in our apartment in New York. We moved when I was six. We lived in New York before we moved to Westchester."

"I didn't know that. Where?"

"East 79th Street. It was in that apartment. I remember the bed. He was lying flat on it. And I peed on his face."

I gasped at the picture I got. "I thought it was on his stomach. I thought you were straddling his stomach."

"No. It was on his face. I wasn't wearing underpants."

I was shocked. My early life had been shocking. My grandfather had molested me. My father's father. I had slept with *her* father. But this was far worse. It was unspeakable.

"Where was your mother?"

"She was there somewhere. It was a big apartment. I might have been three," she conceded. "Who knows? I don't remember the action that prompted me to say that. I must have instantly erased it from my mind."

"Of course you did!" The action was her father licking her vagina. 'That's disgusting."

"He was a sick man," she agreed.

"Disgusting," I repeated. Her father was a pedophile.

"Well, I've made your day," she said sardonically.

"No, I'm very sad," I said.

"I think that's why I got fat. And had no interest in sexuality."

"Of course! That's so sad. It's tragic."

"Not really. It's freeing. I wish I knew how evil he was before he died."

"You did," I said. "You told me he molested your little sister's friends when she had sleepovers."

"No. I didn't know until after. You cried when I told you my father died."

"I did? Not because he died, surely."

"Yes."

"I don't remember that."

"Well I do." Was she evil? Had she always tried to hurt me? Had she fed me to her father on her silver spoon?

"And then you told me the story of you and him," Maddy said.

The past was split like an ovum into rival myths. She had torn the admission out of me on an ordinary Saturday. It had nothing to do with her father's death.

"I wish I had known before," she went on. "I would have acted differently. But I don't know how I would have acted."

"I've been shaken up ever since our last conversation," I admitted the next time we spoke.

"About what?"

"About your father. I thought you had peed on his stomach. How could he do such a thing?"

"But I think he did it out of love," she said.

For a moment, I felt jealous. As if we were rivals, and she was lording it over me.

And then I realized, for the first time, the jealousy she must have felt, having been aroused by her father at three, and knowing that he had slept with me. It was like what my mother had told me right before she died. "You are not the center of the universe!" It wasn't the story of him and me, it was the story of her and him.

That night I lay awake remembering the summer before she moved to California, when I had visited her with my lover. Another artist. We were sitting on the edge of Lake Champlain — Maddy's summer house, across the lake from her mansion in Vermont. Maddy's mother, Doris, was there. She was completely wrinkled from living in Hawaii even though she had just had a facelift.

I was doubled over. I thought I might have to go to the hospital. I was having horrendous cramps. I was about to get my period. I had taken two of every pill I had but nothing worked.

"Here, take this," Doris said. She wore large black-rimmed glasses, Bermuda shorts. The ghost of her pimple still hovered in my mind.

I swallowed the large pill gratefully. Immediately, I was cured.

"I feel all better," I told Maddy at once. "Your mother cured me."

"My mother knows about you and my father," Maddy said.

"How do you know?" I asked, horrified.

"She told me."

I went back to New York haunted by the harm I had done, the pain I had inflicted. I had probably caused their divorce. Then one Saturday morning on the phone, suddenly I decided to ask, "How did your mother find out about your father and me?"

"She never found out," Maddy said. "She doesn't know anything."

She had forgotten her lie.

Later, I found out the single pill her mother had given me was only a

Tylenol Gelcap.

The last time I had seen her had been a year after 9/11. I took a plane on September 11th. There were seats available. She paid for half my fare. She sat at the table in her mother's house and plunged a needle into her stomach. She had diabetes. I had toothache, and abscess. I craved Marinol, the drug I had for chemo but which I needed then for pain. We visited the redwood trees but she collapsed in the woods, and a park vehicle had to come to carry her back to her car. I had brought her two portraits of herself. Oils, that I did with the urgency of Van Gogh painting sunflowers for his dying mother. "My eyes aren't shifty like that," she said. I had to take them back with me on the plane.

An hour later I called back to talk to Tsering, the man from Tibet, who was taking care of her. He said William would be there in a week.

My daughter tried to cheer me up. "She probably lost a hundred pounds. A woman in my building got Alzheimer's and she forgot she liked to eat. She looked great, but then she died," she added.

A week later, when I called, Maddy answered. She sounded crisp, composed, like her old self. "Who is this?" I told her. "Jill?" she said. She had no idea who I was.

"Yes, I called you last week. On your birthday."

"That was nice of you. I guess I missed your call."

She gave me her son's number, reeling off the digits at terrific speed, and then quickly said goodbye and hung up.

When I called William, his Tibetan wife answered, Karma. I had never spoken to her before. She was the Dali Lama's daughter, Maddy had said.

Or maybe I made that up. Everything about Maddy seemed grand like that.

"William isn't here," she said. "He's not allowed to contact me, or I him. We're divorcing. He wasn't very nice to me in the end. Never mind that

I was his teacher's daughter. My father was very highly esteemed. That's how we met. I'm glad I'm done with it. He dragged me into the dirt.

"I feel as if I know you. Maddy spoke of you, her childhood friend. She told me stories about you and her Dad. Is it true that her father molested her?"

"Yes, I think so," I said.

"I took care of her for three months and she told me the same story fifty times a day."

"How did this happen?"

"It was rapid, a rapid descent into Alzheimer's after her fall. She and William are in complete denial. We begged her not to put stones down in her backyard but she wouldn't listen and she slipped on them and fell. She had surgery and bleeding in the brain. Now she can't remember from one minute to the next."

"Did her dog die?"

"Yes. She fed it all day long, strange foods, and he got a stomach problem and died. He was only five."

"At least she has William."

"She and William hate each other. They have the strangest relationship. She warned me not to trust him, because he looks just like her father."

"She said he lost a hundred thousand of her money on the stock market."

"But he made it back, twice over! He told me he thought his mom was going to die soon and he was going to get her money and he wanted a divorce so that I wouldn't benefit."

"Should I go to see her?"

"No. That would just make her more confused. This is the worst disease that can happen to someone with Maddy's personality – who thinks she is better than everyone else." I was startled by this analysis. I had never thought of her that way. "I miss Mom. Maddy," she corrected herself. "I feel sorry for her."

"I do too." It was like the magic slate I had been given as a child.

You wrote on it and then lifted the clinging transparent sheet. All her memories were erased. She was there, large as life, in Santa Rosa, and she was gone.

As soon as I got off the phone, I looked for the silver mermaid pin. Suddenly I valued all the things she had given me even more. The mermaid pin took on enormous importance. I had to put it on. It showed the connection between us. Could I have lost it? It wasn't in my jewelry drawer. I never put things away. It wasn't on my black ruffled jacket. It wasn't on my nubby sweater from Paris. It was gone. Frantic, I searched through all my closets.

When I found it, the next day, one second afterwards I had forgotten where. It was just a pin.

Jill Hoffman, "Mollie," 2013, Oil on canvas, 18" x 24"

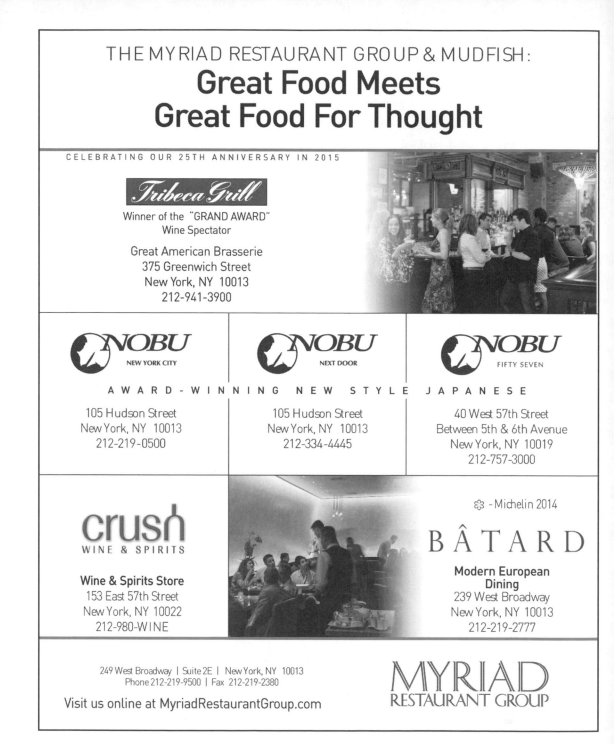

FIND FOOD AND DRINK
OPEN SEVEN DAYS

WALKERS

CORNER OF VARICK & NORTH MOORE
(212) 941-0142   226-9519

THE MUDFISH WORKSHOP

Tuesday or Wednesday 7:30 pm.
Poetry and Fiction
Ongoing since 1990
10 Sessions / $600
212-219-9278

184 Franklin Street, New York, New York 10013

If you take a real crime, the Jennifer Moore murder, add the imagination, insight and humanity of Stephanie Dickinson, you have *Love Highway*. It's as if Stephanie not only has access to diaries of real characters, but to their actual thought processes.

Ted Jonathan, author of *Bones & Jokes*

Stephanie Dickinson's potent new novel ... cuts lines that pierce the vibrancy of love itself—bold, scenic and memorable. *Love Highway* is about those who feed on others' hunger and the value of looking within, no matter how painful.

Jen Knox, author of *Don't Tease the Elephants*

Set in New York City and its outskirts, she gives us the shiny girls who will risk everything to be part of what they've been brainwashed into believing is bright and essential. Dickinson has a dense, lyrical prose style that infiltrates the senses like a walk through a hot-house full of lilies.

Susan Tepper, author of *The Merrill Diaries*

LOVE HIGHWAY

the new novel by

STEPHANIE DICKINSON

SPUYTEN DUYVIL
SPUYTENDUYVIL.NET
ISBN 978-1-941550-16-8
$18.00
230 pages

distributed by
Small Press Distributors

Love Highway

Stephanie Dickinson

anne

graphic art

Anne Lawrence
917 407 3976
www.annewyork.com

book design

graphic identity

promotions

nonprint

MUDFISH INDIVIDUAL POET SERIES

To order copies: www.mudfish.org

Box Turtle Press/Attitude Art Inc.
184 Franklin Street
New York, New York 10013